Big Skills for the Common Core

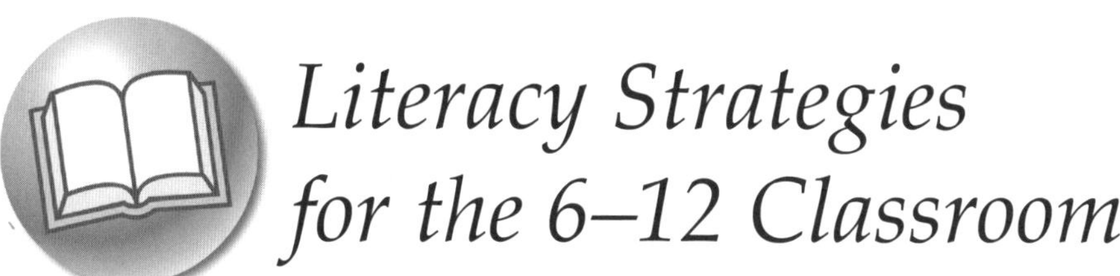

Literacy Strategies for the 6–12 Classroom

Amy Benjamin
with
Michael Hugelmeyer

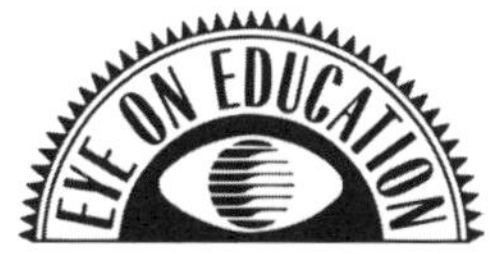

EYE ON EDUCATION
6 DEPOT WAY WEST, SUITE 106
LARCHMONT, NY 10538
(914) 833-0551
(914) 833-0761 fax
www.eyeoneducation.com

Sponsoring Editor: Robert Sickles
Production Editor: Lauren Davis
Copy Editor: Elayne Masters
Designer and Compositor: Bruce Leckie
Cover Designer: Dave Strauss, 3FoldDesign

Library of Congress Cataloging-in-Publication Data

Benjamin, Amy, 1951-
Big skills for the common core : literacy strategies for the 6–12 classroom / Amy Benjamin with Michael Hugelmeyer.
p. cm.
Includes bibliographical references.
ISBN 978-1-59667-231-4
1. Language arts (Secondary)—United States. 2. Language arts (Secondary)—Standards—United States. 3. Language arts—Correlation with content subjects—United States. I. Hugelmeyer, Michael. II. Title.
LB1631.B38 2012
428.0071'2—dc23 2012032464

10 9 8 7 6 5 4 3 2 1

Also Available from Eye On Education

Common Core Literacy Lesson Plans:
Ready-to-Use Resources, K–5
Ed. Lauren Davis

Common Core Literacy Lesson Plans:
Ready-to-Use Resources, 6–8
Ed. Lauren Davis

Common Core Literacy Lesson Plans:
Ready-to-Use Resources, 9–12
Ed. Lauren Davis

Vocabulary at the Core:
Teaching the Common Core Standards
Amy Benjamin and John T. Crow

But I'm Not a Reading Teacher:
Strategies for Literacy Instruction in the Content Areas
Amy Benjamin

Teaching Grammar: What Really Works
Amy Benjamin and Joan Berger

Math in Plain English:
Literacy Strategies for the Mathematics Classroom
Amy Benjamin

Teaching Critical Thinking:
Using Seminars for 21st Century Literacy
Terry Roberts and Laura Billings

Rigor Made Easy:
Getting Started
Barbara R. Blackburn

Rigor Is Not a Four-Letter Word, Second Edition
Barbara R. Blackburn

Acknowledgements

We would like to thank the entire staff at Eye On Education in Larchmont, New York, most especially its president Robert N. Sickles and senior editor Lauren Davis for giving us the opportunity to write this book. We would also like to thank the pre-publication reviewers who gave us careful and thoughtful suggestions for revision. In addition, we are sincerely grateful to the teachers whose exceptional work in the classroom is described in this book: Gary DelCioppo and Sean Buraga, science teachers at Blue Mountain Middle School in Montrose, New York (Hendrick Hudson School District); Patrick Burke, Alison Laino, Jo-Ann Dellaposta, Justin Cobis, Christine Miller, Dena Tishim, and Stephanie Piraino at Riverhead High School in Riverhead, New York; and Dali Rastello, assistant principal at Central Islip High School in New York.

Meet the Authors

After enjoying a long and rewarding career as an English teacher in the Hendrick Hudson School District in Montrose, New York, **Amy Benjamin** now works as a national consultant. Her goal is to improve education by helping teachers recognize the role that language plays in learning. As such, the Common Core State Standards, with their emphasis on literacy as a foundational skill across all subject areas, fits perfectly into her vision of education reform. Amy has been honored for excellence in teaching by Tufts University, Union College, and the New York State English Council. Her classroom was used as a model for standards-based teaching by the New York State Education Department. Amy lives in Dutchess County, New York, with her husband, Howard. Their son, Mitchell, lives in California and works in the television industry. This is the eleventh book that she has written for Eye On Education.

Author **Michael Hugelmeyer** is in his tenth year in the field of education, working as the Assistant Principal at Riverhead High School on Long Island, New York. Before becoming an administrator, he was a social studies teacher and an athletic coach at Glen Cove High School in Glen Cove, New York. Michael began his preparatory work in education as an undergraduate and graduate student at Villanova University. He currently lives on Long Island's East End and is very happily married to Alexis, his wife of six years. They have two beautiful children, Isabella and Lance. This is the first book Michael has written.

Free Downloads

Several of the resources discussed and displayed in this book are also available on Eye On Education's website as Adobe Acrobat files. Permission has been granted to purchasers of this book to download these resources and print them.

You can access these downloads by visiting Eye On Education's website: www.eyeoneducation.com. From the home page, click on FREE, and then click on Supplemental Downloads. Alternatively, you can search or browse our website to find this book, and then click on "Log in to Access Supplemental Downloads."

Your book-buyer access code is **BSC-7231-4**.

Contents

Part 3: Speaking and Listening

Introduction

This book is about the key role that academic skills play in getting students to achieve durable learning in all subject areas. Learning involves facts and concepts, but it *depends* upon skills and strategies. The difference between a skill and a strategy is that a skill is automatic, but a strategy requires conscious thought about how to put a plan into action. When students leave a class, they should leave that class with more than a bunch of facts and figures. They should be continuously using strategies for learning that, through practice, become skills. Using a new word or two, taking notes, finding connections between science and social studies, asking clear questions, conversing with peers and adults about serious subjects: these are skills that need to become automatic through instruction in learning strategies.

Now that the Common Core State Standards (Common Core, for short) have been adopted by most states in the United States, we should take a fresh look at the role that specific academic skills and strategies play in school. While the Competency-Based Education (CBE) movement of the 1970s focused on basic skills, some say at the expense of content, the Common Core emphasizes high-level thinking skills, especially analysis, synthesis, comparison/contrast, and evaluation. This book explains how academic skills are a vehicle for learning content. Content—the facts and figures of education—is easily forgotten unless applied. Skills—making meaning from the content—create durable learning. *Skills magnetize content. Strategies, when practiced, lead to skills.*

The Common Core State Standards

We assume that you know the basics of the Common Core. The standards are divided into two houses: English Language Arts & Literacy in History/Social Studies, Science, and Technical Subjects in one house; Mathematics in the other.

The standards allow us to act locally while thinking globally. Educators are expected to make appropriate choices about what books students will read, what tasks they will do, what words they will learn, how to sequence learning within the school year, etc. The key resource for learning about the Common Core is its website, www.corestandards.org.

Although there are thirty-two standards divided into four sections (reading, writing, speaking and listening, language), the skills are overlapping and interlocking, so there are actually far fewer than thirty-two discrete standards. This book focuses on the branch of the Common Core that deals with literacy, English Language Arts & Literacy in History / Social Studies, Science, and Technical Subjects. Literacy is defined as the ability to read and write. The more we develop our students' listening and speaking skills, the stronger their reading and writing skills will be.

CCR: What Does it Mean to Be "College and Career Ready"?

In the jargon of education, CCR does not stand for Creedence Clearwater Revival. It stands for College and Career Ready. That is the ultimate goal of the Common Core: to ensure that every student holding a diploma from an American high school has the knowledge, attitude, skills, and strategies to further their education on yet a higher level, whether that be at a community college, a four-year college, a technical training institution, the military, or the workplace. It is often said that the students who sit before us today will spend their adult lives doing work as well as social and leisure activities that we cannot even imagine. But whatever their world looks like in the coming decades, we can be certain that they will need to think, to communicate, and—most importantly—to adapt.

We would like to simplify the Common Core by saying that college and career readiness is a matter of *having the skills and strategies that enable us to keep on learning.*

Key Changes and Challenges

Each state has had to examine its existing standards against those of the Common Core for literacy in English language arts, history, social studies, science, and technical subjects. The difference between the two sets of standards is expressed in what is usually called a "crosswalk." Although the crosswalk will vary from state to state, the following tend to be the salient changes and challenges from the old to the new:

- Increased emphasis on **elevating text complexity**, K–12, until students are capable of reading college-level reading materials and career reading materials, such as training manuals and legal documents
- Increased amount of **informational text** (as opposed to narrative text), both in reading and in writing
- Emphasis on writing for the purposes of **argumentation, coherent information, and research; emphasis on citing sources** that justify and provide further references
- Emphasis on **answering questions by locating evidence in the text**, as opposed to giving a personal opinion about the text
- Continuous development of literacy and language skills as **a shared responsibility**, beyond the English language arts classroom
- Use of data derived from **formative assessment**. Formative assessments can be informal and serve to diagnose strengths and weaknesses so that instruction can adapt to students' demonstrated needs.
- Emphasis on depth and development of **higher-order thinking skills** (especially analysis, synthesis, and evaluation), rather than broad but shallow recitation and memorization of facts and figures

Literacy: A Shared Responsibility

For decades, teachers have been encouraged to weave reading and writing instruction into the fabric of how they teach not only English language arts but also social studies, science, mathematics, and technical subjects. "Everybody is a reading teacher and a writing teacher" has become a cliché and thus has lost the power of its meaning. Teachers routinely roll their eyes and say, "Here we go again," when professional development time is devoted to the theme of integrating literacy skills into subjects other than English language arts.

In all fairness, there are teachers, such as those whose practices are described in this book, who do integrate language and literacy skills naturally into content. But there are not enough of these teachers on the secondary level. "I don't have time." "We already do that." "Shouldn't they (the students) have already been taught this?" "That's not my job." These attitudes result in the dismal statistics about the number of college students who enter college in a stumble. "Thirty-four percent of all students at public colleges and universities enroll in at least one remedial course. The number is higher at community colleges; on average, 43 percent of students require remediation" (National Conference of

State Legislatures report, January 2011, p. 1). It is argued that many students who are sent off to noncredit remedial courses on the basis of standardized tests (such as the ACT's Accuplacer) could actually perform satisfactorily in college courses if placement were based on their high school GPAs. However, we still have to wonder why so many American high school graduates fare so poorly on tests of academic skills. And we are left with the sad fact that "only seventeen percent (compared to fifty-eight percent) of students enrolled in remedial reading earn a bachelor's degree" (Alliance for Excellence in Education, quoted in "Reforming Remedial Education, National Conference of State Legislatures).

It is this disconnect between K–12 and college that the "shared responsibility" for literacy skills among educators must remedy. Colleges need better ways of determining who needs remediation in what, as well as how that remediation is best achieved, but our high school graduates do need better literacy skills and strategies. Literacy skills have to be taught, reinforced, and practiced in a way that is rich, pervasive, informed, and aggressive. Here is the Common Core directive:

The Standards insist that instruction in reading, writing, speaking, listening, and language be a shared responsibility within the school (www.corestandards.org).

Interdisciplinary Learning and Skills for the Common Core

Interdisciplinary learning is powerful because it creates connections, reinforcing and amplifying the meaning of content. Also, most real-life tasks are not limited to a single intellectual discipline; we integrate different kinds of knowledge all the time. Yet we educators tend to remain stuck in our own areas of expertise. We are stuck physically, in a single classroom and department, and we tend to be stuck intellectually—limiting the world to the curriculum of the science teacher, the social studies teacher, the English teacher, the mathematics teacher, et al. When we talk to teachers about interdisciplinary learning, we hear responses like "Well, that would be nice, but the timing doesn't work. We teach the Roman Empire in October, but the English department has to share the set of *Julius Caesar* books, so they do the play at different times." Or, "Well, that would be nice, but we spend a good five weeks on *Julius Caesar*, and the social studies people cover Rome in five *days*." In other words, we tend to think about interdisciplinary learning as being only about content.

We propose thinking about building interdisciplinary learning around common *skills* and *strategies*. Regardless of the content, the students can be developing the key skills that we are addressing in this book. These skills coalesce around reading, writing, speaking, and listening, with competence in academic vocabulary infused therein.

Breaking Down the Anchor Standards

The following chart is designed to make it easier for you to process the thirty-two anchor standards. The language of the standards document is clear and familiar; however, because there is so much essential overlap, some people get lost in the verbiage. We've provided a skeletal version in the following tables. We suggest that you review the whole thing, which we assume is already somewhat familiar to you, and then compress your thinking about each standard by using the thumbnails on the left.

We can crystallize all of the anchor standards by saying that we want students to hone the skill of *processing information through language*. Since all of the standards relate to that one goal, you will find that they are deeply connected. To dismiss the connectedness as mere redundancy would be a misunderstanding of the key concept that allows these literacy standards to work in support of, and not in competition with, content learning. That key concept is coherence. A coherent curriculum is one in which the parts are connected. The Common Core connects the parts of a schoolwide curriculum through literacy and language.

Common Core, Grades 6–12: Anchor Standards for READING
English Language Arts & Literacy in History/Social Studies, Science, and Technical Subjects

BIG SKILLS	FULL WORDING FROM THE STANDARDS DOCUMENT
	Key Ideas and Details
1. Read closely.	Read closely to determine what the text says explicitly and to make logical inferences from it; cite specific textual evidence when writing or speaking to support conclusions drawn from the text.
2. Track themes and summarize main ideas.	Determine central ideas or themes of a text and analyze their development; summarize the key supporting details and ideas.
3. Understand and follow progressions.	Analyze how and why individuals, events, and ideas develop and interact over the course of a text.
	Craft and Structure
4. Know what the words/phrases mean in a given context.	Interpret words and phrases as they are used in a text, including determining technical, connotative, and figurative meanings, and analyze how specific word choices shape meaning or tone.

BIG SKILLS	FULL WORDING FROM THE STANDARDS DOCUMENT
5. Analyze how the details contribute to each other and to the overall meaning.	Analyze the structure of texts, including how specific sentences, paragraphs, and larger portions of the text (e.g., a section, chapter, scene, or stanza) relate to each other and the whole.
6. Assess how point of view or purpose affects meaning.	Assess how point of view or purpose shapes the content and style of a text.
Integration of Knowledge and Ideas	
7. Understand charts, graphs, and other numerical and visual information and media in addition to words.	Integrate and evaluate content presented in diverse formats and media, including visually and quantitatively, as well as in words.
8. Judge the validity of arguments.	Delineate and evaluate the argument and specific claims in a text, including the validity of the reasoning as well as the relevance and sufficiency of the evidence.
9. Compare texts that address similar subjects. Consider both content and style.	Analyze how two or more texts address similar themes or topics in order to build knowledge or to compare the approaches the authors take.
Range of Reading and Level of Text Complexity	
10. Comprehend complex text. (Use the exemplars in Appendix B of the Common Core State Standards as a guide for grade-level expectations: www.corestandards.org.)	Read and comprehend complex literary and informational texts independently and proficiently.

Common Core, Grades 6–12: Anchor Standards for WRITING
English Language Arts & Literacy in History/Social Studies, Science, and Technical Subjects

BIG SKILLS	FULL WORDING FROM THE STANDARDS DOCUMENT
Types and Purposes	
1. Write arguments.	Write arguments to support claims in an analysis of substantive topics or texts, using valid reasoning and relevant and sufficient evidence.
2. Write informative/ explanatory texts.	Write informative/explanatory texts to examine and convey complex ideas and information clearly and accurately through the effective selection, organization, and analysis of content.
3. Write narratives.	Write narratives to develop real or imagined experiences or events using effective technique, well-chosen details, and well-structured event sequences.
Production and Distribution	
4. Match your style to the expectations of the audience.	Produce clear and coherent writing in which the development, organization, and style are appropriate to task, purpose, and audience.
5. Use the writing process.	Develop and strengthen writing as needed by planning, revising, editing, rewriting, or trying a new approach.
6. Use technology as a collaborative tool.	Use technology, including the Internet, to produce and publish writing and to interact and collaborate with others.
Research to Build and Present Knowledge	
7. Conduct short as well as more sustained research projects.	Conduct short as well as more sustained research projects based on focused questions, demonstrating understanding of the subject under investigation.
8. Gather information from multiple sources. Judge the accuracy of your sources. Use proper citations. Avoid plagiarism.	Gather relevant information from multiple print and digital sources, assess the credibility and accuracy of each source, and integrate the information while avoiding plagiarism.

BIG SKILLS	FULL WORDING FROM THE STANDARDS DOCUMENT
9. Use both literary and informational texts to support, inform, and enrich your claims.	Draw evidence from literary or informational texts to support analysis, reflection, and research.
Range of Writing	
10. Write routinely; write *both* formally and informally, depending on the expectations of the audience; write polished pieces, revised over time; *also*, write on-demand pieces within a short time frame, such as a single class period; use writing as *both* a means for learning and a way to demonstrate your knowledge.	Write routinely over extended time frames (time for research, reflection, and revision) and shorter time frames (a single sitting or a day or two) for a range of tasks, purposes, and audiences.

Common Core, Grades 6–12:
Anchor Standards for SPEAKING AND LISTENING
English Language Arts

BIG SKILLS	FULL WORDING FROM THE STANDARDS DOCUMENT
Comprehension and Collaboration	
1. Develop socially acceptable conversation skills.	Prepare for and participate effectively in a range of conversations and collaborations with diverse partners, building on others' ideas and expressing their own clearly and persuasively.
2. Verbally summarize information that you've heard or read.	Integrate and evaluate information presented in diverse media and formats, including visually, quantitatively, and orally.
3. Assess the credibility of what you read and hear.	Evaluate a speaker's point of view, reasoning, and use of evidence and rhetoric.

Presentation of Knowledge and Ideas	
4. Present meaningful ideas and information coherently and courteously.	Present information, findings, and supporting evidence such that listeners can follow the line of reasoning and the organization, development, and style are appropriate to task, purpose, and audience.
5. Enhance formal presentations with visuals, including digital media.	Make strategic use of digital media and visual displays of data to express information and enhance understanding of presentations.
6. Know the rules of formal spoken English and apply them when appropriate to the audience.	Adapt speech to a variety of contexts and communicative tasks, demonstrating command of formal English when indicated or appropriate.

Common Core, Grades 6–12: Anchor Standards for LANGUAGE
English Language Arts

BIG SKILLS	FULL WORDING FROM THE STANDARDS DOCUMENT
Conventions of Standard English	
1. Know the rules of formal standard written and spoken English and apply them when your audience expects you to do so. Accurately perceive the circumstances when your audience expects you to use a formal language tone.	Demonstrate command of the conventions of standard English grammar and usage when writing or speaking.
2. The above includes the visuals of writing: capitalization, punctuation, and spelling.	Demonstrate command of the conventions of standard English capitalization, punctuation, and spelling when writing.

BIG SKILLS	FULL WORDING FROM THE STANDARDS DOCUMENT
Knowledge of Language	
3. Understand that language is a changeable social contract. Make effective choices. Expand your understanding of the language choices of others.	Apply knowledge of language to understand how language functions in different contexts, to make effective choices for meaning or style, and to comprehend more fully when reading or listening.
Vocabulary Acquisition and Use	
4. Figure out what new words/phrases mean using context, word parts, dictionaries, and other reference tools.	Determine or clarify the meaning of unknown and multiple-meaning words and phrases by using context clues, analyzing meaningful word parts, and consulting general and specialized reference materials, as appropriate.
5. Understand that words can be nuanced and can have multiple meanings.	Demonstrate understanding of figurative language, word relationships, and nuances in word meanings.
6. Understand and use an academic/businesslike level of language.	Acquire and use accurately a range of general academic and domain-specific words and phrases sufficient for reading, writing, speaking, and listening at the college- and career-readiness level; demonstrate independence in gathering vocabulary knowledge when considering a word or phrase important to comprehension or expression.

Part 1

Reading

CHAPTER 1

Reading and the Common Core

The most significant shift in the instructional implications of the Common Core State Standards is that teachers of all subjects, not just English, are required to actually teach the literacy skills relevant to their content. In the past, although there have been local initiatives and plenty of lip service given to "reading and writing in the content areas," the reality has been that reading comprehension skills have been taught, if at all, by English teachers. Even then, English teachers are not necessarily trained as *reading* teachers. Teachers of other subject areas have expected the literacy skills to be reinforced in English class and then applied to the reading in other classes.

Why bother? Why not leave things as they've been, relying on the primary grades to teach the fundamental decoding skills and phonics and then assuming that once a student can read, she can read anything? Why not continue in the assumption that if a student can study *Hamlet* in English class, she can read the chemistry textbook on her own? In its August 2006 Issue Brief Fact Sheet, The Alliance for Excellent Education (sponsored by MetLife) cites that in addition to the low graduation rate of 70 percent in American high schools, about 50 percent of those who do graduate are not capable of handling college-level work. And we all know, college work is primarily reading as well as writing that is based on reading. "Analyses of students' preparation for college-level work show the weakness of core skills, such as basic study habits and the ability to understand and manage complicated material. The lack of preparation is also apparent in multiple subject areas; of college freshmen taking remedial courses" (Alliance 2006 Fact Sheet). Two-thirds of students taking remedial courses in college are taking them in reading and/or writing. One of the main purposes of the standards is to bridge the skills gap between high school graduates and college freshmen. The gap has everything to do with the reading capacity of students when they graduate from high school:

> Research shows that the leading predictor that a student will drop of out college is the need for remedial reading. While 58 percent of students who take no remedial education courses earn a bachelor's degree within eight years, only 17 percent of students who enroll in a remedial reading course receive a BS or BA within the same period. (Alliance 2006 Fact Sheet)

The first set of standards addresses reading, emphasizing that over the years of their education, students need to build capacity to read increasingly complex text in various genres. They need a repertoire of reading strategies that accommodate a range of texts and purposes for reading.

You will see immediately that the standards for the secondary grade levels are about comprehension, not such fundamentals as decoding, phonics, and basic fluency.

Below are simplified statements of the standards, followed by the original language (www.corestandards.org).

Breaking Down the Standards

Key Ideas and Details

1. **Read closely.** Read closely to determine what the text says explicitly and to make logical inferences from it; cite specific textual evidence when writing or speaking to support conclusions drawn from text.

2. **Track themes and summarize main ideas.** Determine central ideas or themes of a text and analyze their development; summarize the key supporting details and ideas.

3. **Understand and follow progressions.** Analyze how and why individuals, events, and ideas develop and interact over the course of a text.

Craft and Structure

4. **Know what the words and phrases mean in a given context.** Interpret words and phrases as they are used in a text, determining technical, connotative, and figurative meanings, and analyze how specific word choices shape meaning or tone.

5. **Analyze how the details contribute to each other and to the overall meaning.** Analyze the structure of texts, including how specific sentences, paragraphs, and larger portions of text (e.g. section, chapter, scene, or stanza) relate to each other and the whole.

6. **Assess how point of view or purpose affects meaning.** Assess how point of view or purpose shapes the content and style of text.

Integration of Knowledge and Ideas

7. **Understand charts, graphs, and other numerical information and media in addition to just the words.** Integrate and evaluate content presented in diverse formats and media, including visually and quantitatively, as well as in words.

8. **Judge the validity of arguments.** Delineate and evaluate the arguments and specific claims in a text, including the validity of the reasoning as well as the relevance and sufficiency of the evidence.

9. **Compare texts that address similar subjects.** Consider both content and style. Analyze how two or more texts address similar themes or topics in order to build knowledge or compare the approaches the authors take.

Range of Reading and Level of Text Complexity

10. **Comprehend complex text.** Use exemplars in Appendix B of the Common Core State Standards as a guide for grade-level expectations (www.corestandards.org).

Regarding the range and content of the Reading Standards, the Common Core State Standards document (www.corestandards.org) says this:

> To become college and career ready, students must grapple with works of exceptional craft and thought whose range extends across genres, cultures, and centuries. Such works offer profound insights into the human condition and serve as models for students' own thinking and writing. Along with high-quality contemporary works, these texts should be chosen from among seminal U.S. documents, the classics of American literature, and the timeless dramas of Shakespeare. Through wide and deep reading of literature and literary nonfiction of steadily increasing sophistication, students gain a reservoir of literary and cultural knowledge, references, and images; the ability to evaluate intricate arguments; and the capacity to surmount the challenge posed by complex texts. (p. 35)

This section will address two modes of reading. Both are necessary to achieve full competency for college and career survival. The first mode we will discuss is *meticulous reading of a range of increasingly complex text*. By this, we mean the kind of challenging reading that makes significant demands on the reader's patience, determination, concentration, and time. The second mode is *recreational reading*. Recreational reading is fundamental to building the kind of background knowledge and automatic functioning to develop the cognitive strength necessary for the other mode. There are occasions in school and in the workplace when it is advisable to skim, scan, or sample a text rather than read every word. The features of the text—headings, summaries, pictures, graphics, introductions—assist the reader in getting the gist. Sometimes, the gist is all we need. Other times, we need to skim a chapter to establish sufficient background knowledge so that the details can stick to something in our heads before we go on to read the whole piece. Full competence is achieved through practice in recreational reading of text that is easy for the reader and meticulous reading of text that is difficult for the reader.

It is important to understand that both modes—meticulous and recreational reading—are necessary to build full competence. The two modes are interdependent. Either of them will strengthen the other, but the absence of practice in either will weaken both. All teachers need to determine how they can incorporate both meticulous and recreational reading.

CHAPTER 2

Meticulous Reading

William Faulkner was once asked to give his advice to readers of his fiction who couldn't understand it even after reading it three times. Faulkner's advice: "Read it four times."

The standards require progressive levels of reading comprehension in a variety of texts. As they advance through K–12 education, students are expected to deepen their comprehension and handle longer and more complex text in a variety of genres, adapting their reading pace to suit specific purposes. For the classroom teacher, this means that students need to be reading more, reading progressively complex text, and knowing how and when to speed up, slow down, reread, get the gist, read between the lines, take notes, take a break, and make whatever mental and environmental adjustments they need to make to facilitate comprehension.

A powerful, if overused, verb that the Common Core uses is *grapple*: "Students must *grapple* with works of exceptional craft and thought" (College and Career Readiness Anchor Standards for Reading, p. 35, www.corestandards.org). The metaphor "staircase of complexity" represents the increasing demands that we should be making on readers as they go through the years of complexity. Admittedly, it didn't take long for *grapple* and *staircase of complexity* to become clichés in the education world, but we'll ask your indulgence as we sparingly use these terms in this chapter.

What exactly does it mean to have to *grapple* with text? It means, first and foremost, that the reader has to be in an environment and state of mind conducive to focusing, "suiting up," so to speak. That is why for many students, the only place where meticulous reading of complex text takes place is within the walls of the school. Outside of school, an environment for concentration on serious reading may not be available. Despite the fact that some people swear they can read perfectly well in the midst of music, ambient conversation, television, or waiting in line at the deli, we contend that there's a unique energy that comes to life only in quiet. This energy has been compared to putting an ear to a seashell. To hear the book in your mind's ear, along with your own sense-making inner monologue, it has to be quiet. There's no denying that the brain has to work to block out competing noise. The mind is drawn to comprehensible input. The rhythms of music and the words of conversation easily snuff out the fragile inner voice of the reader.

To grapple with text is to reread as necessary. Rereading to build comprehension results from self-monitoring—having, and heeding, the inner voice that confirms or questions full comprehension. Grappling with complex text does not happen in a linear way. Intervening thoughts, conversations, and actions construct meaning out of the text, and, in literary text, that meaning can grow richer as we experience life and revisit it.

To grapple with text is to use outside resources. We'll designate three categories of outside resources. The first is the reading buddy, a peer who may be as lost as you. However, between the two of you, you can converse your way into understanding. I (Amy) love Shakespeare, but I always have a hard time understanding either the text or a performance at my first exposure to a play. I watched the film version of Richard III at home with my sister, and we paused it frequently to talk about what was happening and to make sure we understood before going on. That is what grappling with text looks like. Having a reading buddy is also motivating, as you and that person have agreed as friends to help each other. That is why in higher education a key strategy is the formation of a study group. The second outside resource might be a reference tool: a dictionary, an abstract or summary (scientific papers offer an abstract up front so you have a schema on which to hang the details), or encyclopedic information that provides needed background.

Finally, to grapple with text is to use informal writing as a means to concentrate to understand: marking the text, outlining, summarizing, listing. All of these are strategies of active reading, the purposeful building of understanding by actually doing something beyond letting your eyes wander over the page, hoping the test won't be hard. Active readers set up the reading environment to maximize their concentration; they enter the text with a purpose and with requisite background knowledge; they continuously predict and confirm; they monitor their comprehension and read recursively; they adjust their pace; they use resources; they interact with the text; they consider who the author is; they read in accordance with the genre; and they socialize the learning process. Passive readers do not do these things, either because they don't know about them, don't believe they will work, or have other learning interference issues that hold them back. Our job is to continually challenge students to read at a higher level than they thought they could, and to provide the class time and place for them to socialize the learning process. Our job is to be knowledgeable and to model our own internal processes as we *also* work to extract meaning from difficult text.

TIP: Strategies for Grappling With a Challenging Text

- Be somewhere you can concentrate.
- Reread as necessary.
- Use outside resources, such as a reading buddy and/or a reference tool.
- Use informal writing as a means to concentrate to understand: marking the text, outlining, summarizing, listing.

What Defines Text Complexity?

There are no precise measures of text complexity. It used to be measured by two factors: sentence length and word length. Clearly, that is an inaccurate, if broadly useful, way to determine how much brainpower it takes to comprehend something that we read. But the authors of the Common Core have done an admirable job of delineating what kinds of factors go into determining text complexity. In addition to those two quantitative measures (sentence length and word length), we now have a better idea of some qualitative features that go into the mix, such as subtleties, author's assumptions about the reader, eye appeal, vocabulary, level of abstraction, and era in which the text was written.

- **Subtleties.** Are there layers of meaning? Is it possible to derive new meaning from reading the text more than once? Is there symbolism? Figurative language? Wordplay?
- **Author's assumptions about the reader.** How much background knowledge does the author assume that the reader has?
- **Eye appeal.** Does the physical layout of the text (also called *text features*) make it easier or more challenging for the reader? Are there pictures? Is there symbolic and numerical information, such as graphs, tables, and charts? If so, sometimes this kind of information is translated clearly into words anyway, so the reader actually has a choice of how to process the

information. Other times, the reader is expected to interpret the graphic information, and will not be able to comprehend the information without examining it carefully.

- **Vocabulary.** How rare are the words? In the case of rare words, how necessary is it to understand them in order to get a gist of the text? Does the author provide contextual clues to the meaning of unfamiliar words? Are these words that can be broken down into components (prefix, root, suffix) that the reader knows? Are unfamiliar words repeated? (This can be either a help or a hindrance, depending on whether the reader can figure out the word in multiple contexts, or whether she has stopped to find its meaning.) Remember that a reader who stops, even briefly, to consult an outside source for a word's meaning has to break the flow of comprehension.

- **Level of abstraction.** The less we can picture and touch something, the more difficult it is to understand it, let alone the subtleties and details of it. Processes, concepts, theories, and systems of organization are examples of abstractions. Certain word endings create abstract concepts. When you see a lot of words ending in *-tion, -ity, -ment, -ism, -ness, -acy*, you know you are in Abstraction Land. Interestingly, the world of fiction (narrative and literary text) is populated by people, things, and specific actions. These people, things, and actions are usually vividly described with adjectives and adverbs. Hence, stories tend to be concrete (and easy to visualize) rather than abstract (not so easy to visualize). This is one of the reasons students with limited experience in a wide variety of text often find it difficult to comprehend science text even though they have always been good at reading narrative text.

- **Era in which the text was written.** Was it written before the twentieth century? If so, the style is likely to have archaic words, long sentences, long paragraphs, and unfamiliar references to nouns (things no longer in use). Even text written before the middle of the twentieth century can be challenging. Language changes surprisingly fast, and today's student may be unfamiliar with the sentence styles and nouns of not too long ago.

The Common Core emphasizes that students should be able to comprehend America's founding documents, such as the Declaration of Independence, the Constitution, and key speeches that led to the American Revolution. The language of such documents includes all kinds of embedded clauses, long sentences, pronouns that are not near their referents, and other features of complex—more importantly, unfamiliar—writing style.

TIP: Understanding Informational Texts vs. Literary Nonfiction

There are two kinds of nonfiction. Text whose purpose is to lay out information purely for its own sake—textbooks, reports, straight news articles, encyclopedic information—we will designate as strictly informational text. Strictly informational text is highly organized, often marked by headings and subheadings, and does not digress. Strictly informational text falls easily into an outline form, which is why outlining is an excellent way of processing, reviewing, and remembering it.

Then we have literary nonfiction—memoirs, lyric poetry, editorials and essays, biographies that are meant to be read as stories (rather than encyclopedia entries), nature writing, and letters. These are crafted with rhetorical flourishes and offer more than mere information. They are meant to be savored for the beauty and power of the language that composes the information, not just for the information.

The Common Core reading standards require that students gather experience in both types of nonfiction. This means that English teachers must include some strictly informational text to supplement the literary pieces, *and* that content-area teachers must supplement the textbook-type information with a few literary pieces.

Becoming a Meticulous Reader: Practice and Strategies

The foundations for becoming a skillful reader are built through practice in reading a variety of texts. It's practice that provides the habitual reader with sufficient exposures to new vocabulary. It also builds stamina to concentrate for longer periods of time, to take in words in groups (rather than singly, as unpracticed readers have to do because they can't anticipate how words are going to be used in phrases), and to create that critical mass of background knowledge that facilitates comprehension more than anything else. So, first and foremost, students need practice in reading academic text. They need daily practice, and they need it throughout each day.

But very few students practice reading *enough* to become as skillful as they need to be without explicit instruction in comprehension strategies. Let's remember, as we go through some strategies, that strategies can only supplement practice—you cannot dispense with practice in favor of learning strategies. But it might actually work to do the reverse, that is, dispense with the strategy instruction and rely wholly on practice to create skillful readers. Most habitual readers teach themselves strategies in the course of doing whatever comes naturally to create meaning from text. That is because they are motivated. In the absence of sufficient practice (which would inculcate the strategies naturally), we can do our best to explain and demonstrate the behaviors and mental habits of skillful readers.

By *strategies*, we mean "methods or procedures that readers more or less apply intentionally to adequately process and understand the information presented in a text" (Poole, p. 3). We know that skillful readers do employ a variety of strategies, while poor readers do not. Skillful readers have a high degree of self-awareness when it comes to reading. They know what they need as readers, they are aware of when comprehension breaks down, and they actively repair—usually rereading, seeking a resource, or even just changing the environment to a more conducive one for reading—when they do not comprehend. They have a mental reading toolbox and they use it. Unskilled readers may have once received such a toolbox, but they left it in their lockers, and half the tools are still in the original packaging. As with any set of tools, we don't become an expert because we have a set of tools. We become an expert because we do the activity, and in doing it, we learn how, when, and why to use the tools.

We divide reading strategies into two categories: those that are internal, taking place entirely in the mind of the reader and therefore not observable or measurable, and those that are external, which can be observed and measured.

Michaela is a sixth grader. She has to read a biography about a person who won a Nobel Prize.

1. **Selecting the right book for herself (internal and external).** The school librarian has carted some books that she thought the sixth graders would find interesting. The class comes in for their weekly library time, and the librarian gives a little book talk on a few of the Nobel Prize winners and the books about them. Michaela kicks the tires of a few of them and decides on a book about the social reformer Jane Addams. Her decision is based on her interest in getting to know how and why Jane Addams helped the poor in Chicago, but the fact that the book looks reader-friendly is no small part of her decision.

2. **Making a day-to-day reading budget (external).** Michaela's teacher gives the class a little math problem. Given the time it takes them to read one page and given the number of pages in the book and the number of days a week that they can set aside time to read, how many pages do they need to read each day? That is their reading budget.

3. **Prereading (external).** When the students return to class with the books they selected, the teacher gives each student a large index card, which is to be used as a bookmark. They are to write their reading budgets on one side of the index card. On the other, they are to write five questions that

they hope their book will answer. The teacher explains that these are to be important questions, the kinds of questions that require more than a one- or two-word answer. She gives examples of appropriate questions. (*How did Albert Einstein come up with his ideas?* not *Where was Albert Einstein born?*)

4. **While reading (internal).** Michaela knows that she cannot read amid distractions, such as television, so she finds a quiet place to read (internal). She has found pictures of Jane Addams' Hull House and the Chicago streets, factories, and tenements of Addams' life (external). She visualizes these scenes as she reads (internal). When she's not understanding something, she rereads it (internal). She comes across many words she has not seen before, but she tries to keep reading anyway so as not to lose momentum. If an unknown word really stands in the way of comprehension, Michaela asks her mother for help (external).

5. **After reading (external).** In class, Michaela works with a reading group. Although the sixth-graders are each reading different books, they have a set of universal questions that they answer orally every few days.

Unison Reading: An Effective Approach to Teaching Meticulous Reading

Unison Reading, as developed by Cynthia McCallister (www.learningcultures.com and *Unison Reading: Socially Inclusive Group Instruction for Equity and Achievement*, Corwin, 2011), is a structure for small groups of students to put their voices and heads together to read and understand what they are reading in class. The class is assembled into clusters of readers who have selected a source of information, such as one of several textbooks available. The students have ready access to an appropriate dictionary and preferably a computer or an iPad. At the count of three, the group reads in unison. At the end of each paragraph, the leader asks, "Does everyone understand? (Pause.) Are you sure?" When there are questions about a word meaning, the intent of the text, or anything else related to meaning, the group investigates. Then it's *one-two-three read* the next paragraph. The model is engaging, nonthreatening, and empowering.

Unison Reading reminds me of the music lessons I (Amy) had in school. I played the clarinet, and weekly lessons consisted of a group of three to five other clarinet players. Having been assigned the same sheet music and etudes, we'd practice the piece in unison. When someone would go astray, we'd stop, find the mistake, clarify the problem, and replay. The system was motivating without being too stressful. The playing of the others in the group was empowering. Although I was listening and playing simultaneously, somehow the notes of the others facilitated my ability to anticipate my upcoming notes and perceive the musical pattern. So it is with unison reading. The reading voices blend to give life to the text.

Sentences to Be Reckoned With (And How to Reckon With Them)

Because the biggest stumbling block to comprehension is unfamiliar vocabulary (or familiar words used in unfamiliar ways), we may overlook how syntax—complex ways in which words are put together grammatically—can also block comprehension. Longer sentences are more difficult to process than shorter sentences, but there's more to it than that. The reader needs to find relationships between words, phrases, and clauses in any sentence, and the longer the sentence is, the more likely it is that those relationships will be complicated. There may be a main idea interrupted by one or more subordinating ideas. Very complex sentences—sentences having multiple independent clauses *and* subordinate clauses—are like Russian nesting dolls, structures functioning within structures.

Pre-twentieth century sentences—informational or narrative—can be long compared to modern text, and archaic vocabulary and syntactical styles can add to the confusion. Students need practice and strategies to handle such challenges. Here are a few strategies for reckoning and wrestling with long sentences:

- **The subject-verb strategy.** When reading long sentences, link the subject to the verb. This will foreground the core meaning of the sentence. Long sentences usually separate the subject from the verb with lots of modifiers and even whole clauses. We need to bring forth the core meaning of the sentence by ignoring the modifiers until we grasp the core nouns and verbs. In literary text, we often find inversions, where the subject is placed after the predicate. The sentence becomes clear when we locate the subject and mentally place it in front of the verb. For example, the sentence "Away from light steals home my heavy son" from *Romeo and Juliet* snaps into place when we untangle it: *My heavy* (heavy: full of worry) *son steals* (steals: sneaks) *home, away from light*.

- **The *and-but-so* strategy.** Mark the connective words. These words guide you through the construction of the argument. The simplest of the connectors are *and*, *but*, and *so*. As we move up the staircase of complexity, we find more academic-sounding connectives such as *in addition*, *furthermore*, and *moreover*. Higher on the staircase are *however*, *in contrast*, *on the other hand, on the contrary, nevertheless,* and *even so*. Even higher are *therefore, as a result, because*. You'll find that once the connectives are highlighted, the sentence is much easier to follow.

- **The punctuation strategy.** When reading long sentences, understand that punctuation marks are not just there to follow arbitrary rules. To ignore or misread punctuation is to suffer the collision of words that the punctuation exists to prevent. Longer sentences are likely to have those lesser-used marks of punctuation:
  - **Multiple commas.** Commas create groupings. Allow the comma do its job of grouping words. Once you get the meaning of a grouping, proceed to the next.
  - **Semicolons.** A semicolon signals one of two things. Usually, the semicolon should be read much like a period except that the complete sentences it separates must be related. Process the complete sentences before proceeding. By joining complete sentences with a semicolon and not dividing them with a period, an author is telling you to notice the close relationship between the clauses. The rarer use of a semicolon is to separate items in a series when the items themselves contain commas. The effect is the same in both cases. Think of the semicolon as a Yield sign on the highway and give it a serious pause, just short of a full stop.
  - **Colons.** Although very few students ever use a colon in their own writing, the colon is extremely helpful to the reader. The colon introduces information that will clarify what has previously been stated. When you see a colon, know that the author is about to restate, give example(s) or express an important point in strong, clear language.
  - **Parentheses.** Authors use parentheses to prevent the parenthetical information from getting in the way of understanding the main part of the sentence. First try to get the gist of the sentence without the parenthetical information, and then add that information to your understanding. Realize that parenthetical information is tangential to the essential meaning.
- **The pronoun strategy.** Pronouns are always abstract. That is, they always represent something that has gone before and that the writer expects you to know. When you don't know what a pronoun represents, you cannot comprehend. You must track down its antecedent (that to which the pronoun refers).

Taking/Teaching Reading Comprehension Tests

If we are concerned (which we are) about reading comprehension tests, we need to teach students to anticipate the kinds of questions usually asked on these tests. Skillful test-takers read the passages with these question types in mind, so the questions are not a surprise to them. Typically, reading comprehension tests are multiple choice, with the questions falling into these broad categories.

1. **The "best title" question.** In any reading comprehension test, you can count on seeing a main idea question. The best title is a favorite way to see if the reader can put the whole passage together under a title that captures its main idea. Giving students practice writing titles for passages in informational articles or headlines for newspaper articles is the best way to prepare them for this kind of question.

2. **The "author's purpose" question.** This question is slightly different from the main-idea question in that it focuses more on how the author *delivers* the information instead of what the information actually *consists* of. The "author's purpose" question usually wants the reader to differentiate among broad categories of rhetorical purposes: to explain (or inform), to persuade, or to entertain (see Figure 2.1). More sophisticated questions will call for the reader to discern among more subtle purposes.

Figure 2.1. Author's Purpose

Purpose	Examples
Explain/inform	explore, examine, analyze, describe, define, illuminate, give examples of, present
Persuade	convince, argue, give reasons for, encourage, discourage, promote, refute, make a case for/against, propose
Entertain	amuse, tell a story about, relate the story of

The "best title" and "author's purpose" question types want the reader to consider the passage as a whole. The next two question types ask the reader to consider how specific parts of the passage contribute to its meaning.

3. **The "why is this part here?" question.** This kind of question wants to know if the reader can put the parts together. Perhaps the passage contains an anecdote that is there to allow the reader to personalize the main point. Perhaps there is a visual that is there to elicit an emotional response

from the reader. Perhaps a sentence is there to restate a point in simpler language. Perhaps the closing paragraph repeats an image presented in the first paragraph to give the piece unity. Perhaps a word or phrase is repeated for dramatic effect.

4. **The "vocabulary in context" question.** Like the main idea question, you can count on the vocabulary question. For these questions, the reader needs to rely on the context, not necessarily the traditional or literal meaning of the word. There will be sufficient context to answer the question. A good way to prepare for the vocabulary in context question is to have students read the passage and anticipate the words or phrases that are used in a way that only the context can explain.

The third category of reading comprehension questions is the most subtle. These are inference questions, which require the reader to transcend the literal words of the passage.

5. **These questions are about what the passage *suggests*.** The reader has to be adept at feeling the connotations of words and figurative language. The word *implies* often appears in the question.

6. **These questions are about the author's tone or attitude.** Almost always, the reader is expected to perceive irony or mockery in the author's words. Students need to be trained to recognize irony when what the author is proposing or purporting seems extreme. Although students have no problem recognizing ironic intent on television skits, they often do not expect to encounter irony on a reading comprehension test. Recognizing irony requires significant background knowledge.

The least effective way to prepare students for a reading comprehension test would be to have them do practice tests on their own and then "go over" the test while students "check their answers." Doing that would do little more than predict how students would fare on the actual test. A better way would be to have students work together, problem-solving out loud. Another way would be to have students work together to construct questions of the different types, and then exchange.

It is important to remember that the most significant variable in a reading comprehension test is not the type of questions but the level of complexity of the text. Practicing main-idea questions or inference questions on unchallenging text is not going to help. The best thing we can do to improve student performance on reading comprehension tests is to have them read, reread, talk about, and write about text that demands that they slow down, think, reread, and apply strategies.

CHAPTER 3

Recreational Reading: The Missing Ingredient

Literacy skills—comprehension, speed and accuracy in decoding (fluency), vocabulary development and flexibility, development of a mature writing style—these skills come flowing in by two streams: immersion in print *and* direct instruction. If I had to choose one or the other, I'd go with immersion in print. I don't mean taking a bath in ink (I wish it were that easy). I mean sticking one's nose in a book and turning the pages, not because someone is holding your head underwater until you read but because you actually want to turn the pages. The reader is curious to know what happens next in the story or what information is about to be presented about an interesting topic. Recreational reading is correlated with higher academic achievement, and although we can argue about whether recreational reading is the cause of or the result of good reading skills, we cannot argue about this: good readers do read a lot and get better at it as they do so. Not only that, but recreational readers accrue an increasing amount of other benefits. They are better at writing, spelling, grammar, and vocabulary. They know more about the world than non-readers (Krashen, p. 17).

While even recreational readers need direct instruction in reading strategies (including guided practice) for specific kinds of texts, strategy instruction in the absence of substantial practice in reading (i.e., recreational reading) will never establish the momentum derived from being an actual self-motivated, voluntary reader. It is that momentum that strengthens the cognitive muscles of reading. To be better at reading, you have to *read a lot*. To read a lot, you have to *want* to read a lot. To want to read a lot, you have to have *access to interesting reading material.* In his book *Readicide,* Kelly Gallagher makes the case for immersing K–12 students in a "book flood." "We must start all discussions about the state of reading on our campuses with a simple, direct question: *Do our students have ample access to high-interest reading materials?*" (Gallagher, p. 32).

In the primary and elementary grades, students are usually given a rich array of reading materials and the time and space in school to read them. Most elementary classrooms that we've seen are graced with classroom libraries. Elementary school librarians usually do an admirable job of making their libraries the heart of the school. Elementary schools have book fairs, posters of appealing books, book clubs, and other ways of inviting children into the world of books. Sustained silent reading (SSR) time is often in place. There are even parent-outreach programs that educate parents on the benefits of having books in the home. Additionally, schools seek donations and conduct drives to get books into students' homes.

At the middle school, aggressive encouragement for recreational reading is spottier though still present. But at the high school level, what happens? Typically, reading is consigned to academics, not recreation. English teachers at the high school level usually limit what students read within the confines of their classrooms to assigned reading of the classics. We're fans of the classics, but we strongly believe that a truly effective reading curriculum makes room for books of choice. As for classes other than English, recreational reading related to the subject matter is practically unheard of. Case in point: I've never heard of a school that requires summer reading in any subject other than English. Is that to say that literary fiction is the only kind of reading that students should be doing—or might want to do—over the summer?

Becoming a Lifelong Reader

If a student does not catch the reading bug by the time she gets to high school, it isn't too late! I'm living proof of that. Here's my (Amy's) biblio-autobiography. I grew up in what you'd call a blue-collar family and environment. My parents were recreational readers. We did not have shelves lined with books. There were never more than one or two books lying around, always with bookmarks. My parents believed in the public library and in passing books around among friends. And, yes, in the suburbs of New York in those days, not every split-level house was supplied with a car during the day while Dad took the family car to work. So the bookmobile came around once a week. The Real Housewives of Long Island, circa 1965, would clamber on to it, checking out the latest best-seller. Sidney Sheldon, Harrold Robbins, Jacqueline Susann, Mario Puzo, and, yes, Henry Miller. All this juicy "trash" around, and I had no interest. No patience.

My mother would cajole me to read all the time, pointing out that it was a good hobby, giving you something to talk about with friends, giving you a way to pass the time (aka, getting you out of the kitchen while I'm trying to make dinner). "Go look at Daddy," she would say. "He's reading. No one is making him read. He's reading because he likes to. Why can't you do that once in a while?" My parents did all the right things, but somewhere after *On Beyond Zebra*, I decided I didn't like to read. My grades in school were anemic, and that embarrassed me because I kept the company of friends whose grades were stellar. They read Nancy Drew mysteries one after the other. I tried, but I couldn't get into them. When my most admired friends moved on to Ian Fleming's James Bond series, devouring them like olives, I couldn't see what the fuss was all about.

When I was in the seventh grade, I had a teacher who gave out a reading list from which we could choose. On this reading list were titles like *Moby Dick, Scaramouche, Ivanhoe, Wuthering Heights*. Just the kind of books perfect for a literaphobe like me. That book list really did a lot to ignite my love of reading. What twelve-year-old girl whose favorite half hour a week was *The Beverly Hillbillies* wouldn't want to delve into 400-plus pages of Sir Walter Scott?

Then in the tenth grade (1967—get the picture?), I had a young, idealistic English teacher who apparently recognized in me some budding social consciousness. She handed me a dog-eared paperback before class one day and said, "Here, Amy. Read this and tell me what you think." Well, she was a nice lady, and it was obvious that she believed she could accomplish some good in the world by teaching English. I liked her, but there was no way in this world that I was ever going to read a book a teacher recommended to me. After a polite period of time, I gently returned it and thanked her. "What did you think?" she asked, smiling like the cat that ate the canary. "It was nice," I replied. (The book, by the way, was *The Feminine Mystique* by Betty Friedan, and in case you don't know—which you should—it was that book that launched the Women's Movement. I told her it was nice.)

Not long after that (I was fifteen), I read the book that was to be what Jim Trelease calls my "home run." I'd like to tell you that the book was something romantically grand like *Anna Karenina*, or something girlishly charming like *Little Women*, or even something coming-of-age-with-a-little-edge like *A Tree Grows in Brooklyn*. But my home run book was Sammy Davis Jr.'s cheesy celeb-bio, *Yes I Can*.

I never would have encountered this book had my parents not been including reading for pleasure in their lives. Had *Yes I Can* not been within arm's reach, I would never have discovered a love for reading.

The point of my story is that my becoming a lifelong reader was the result of one thing: access to interesting reading material. Julius Caesar turned down the crown three times, as Shakespeare tells it. Maybe he would have finally changed his mind. Who can argue that access to reading material that is interesting to students creates a greater chance that students will find their home-run books and change their lives? The access cannot end just because students are in high school.

There are some who believe that class time that is not spent listening to a teacher is suspect. They concede that reading is good, that their students are not doing nearly enough of it, and if they did more of it, their skills would improve across the board. But, they argue, shouldn't this recreational reading be done "on the student's own time"? Here is how Jim Trelease (2009) counters this fallacious argument.

> The most at-risk students come from the homes where there is the least opportunity to read for pleasure. More than two decades of NAEP research funded by the U.S. Department of Education clearly shows these students have the fewest books, magazines, and newspapers, and their families watch the most hours of television per day. They are more apt to have televisions in their bedrooms, rooms they share with more than one sibling. They also come from the neighborhoods where their libraries are the worst funded, have the most meager collections, and are open the fewest hours. (www.trelease-on-reading.com)

Stephen D. Krashen (2004) asserts,

> Free voluntary reading (FVR) is one of the most powerful tools we have in language education, and … is the missing ingredient in language arts … . It will not, by itself, produce the highest levels of competence; rather, it provides a foundation so that higher levels of proficiency may be reached. When free voluntary reading is missing, these advanced levels are extremely difficult to attain. (Krashen, *The Power of Reading*, p. 17)

Conclusion: Reading

Reading, both meticulous reading and recreational reading, needs to be a staple in every classroom for the Common Core to be achieved. By reading, we don't mean just *assigning* reading, expecting it to be done for homework.

Let's say you've decided to get serious about exercise. You join the gym and you actually go there to work out. You even hire a personal trainer. Imagine if your trainer just sat you down and told you all about the exercises you should be doing, showed you videos of how people use the machines, and tested you on your knowledge of the weights. Yet, that's about the size of it when we don't actually have students reading in class as part of their learning.

The balance between recreational and meticulous reading of increasingly complex text corresponds to the balance we all need between doing the kind of exercise that is easy and enjoyable, but also strengthening ourselves with those sit-ups and push-ups that are less fun, but necessary.

The four Classroom Close-Ups that follow illustrate ways that excellent teachers infuse reading into classroom practice in various subjects.

CLASSROOM CLOSE-UPS for Reading

The Three-Minute Drill

Patrick Burke is an innovative and enthusiastic social studies teacher with whom I (Michael) often discuss instruction. Our conversations center around what works and what doesn't work to develop the academic skill set of students. He employs a series of instructional strategies that comport with many of the anchor Common Core State Standards for Literacy, including the Three-Minute Drill, which he describes below.

> Over the years, I have observed that my students try to copy everything that appears on the board or PowerPoint slide or to write everything that is said in a class lecture. I would watch and be amazed as to how much the students would write, yet how little they retained. My three-minute drill was originally designed to address this issue. It is a note-taking strategy that incorporates listening, processing, sharing, and summarizing. The drill, similar to a think-pair-share, requires the students to listen to the instructor and to recall the important facts while addressing an essential question. Students share their facts with the person sitting next to them and share back to the teacher, who then summarizes the information to ensure that all of the key points were addressed.
>
> At first, the drill was designed to go along with a study guide that would focus students on the content. However, as the three-minute drill evolved, I found myself using its structure for reading comprehension, charts, graphs, and quotation analysis. Here's how it works.
>
> The key is an oversized hourglass filled with three minutes worth of sand. This prop is great. The students like seeing the sand slowly trickle down, and they almost race to beat it as they write their last fact. (For this example, let us use the discipline of Grade 10 global studies concentrating on the Industrial Revolution unit). I start by explaining the first slide, pointing out the capitalized and/or underlined words (in this case, information on the development of industry in Great Britain). I ask the students to formulate a question based on the slide. I ask them to think of a theme-based question, as opposed to a trivial, detail-oriented question. We're looking for something that addresses the big picture (for example: In the nineteenth century, how was Great Britain's environment conducive to launching the Industrial Revolution?).

> I elicit a few of the students' suggestions, and, once a question is agreed upon, everyone writes that question down. After that, I ask them to put their pens down and just listen. I delve into the explanation, pointing out the facts, without answering the question directly; usually there are two to three slides to go along with this mini-lecture.
>
> Then, I turn the hourglass over and say, "You now have three minutes to answer our essential question. Use the facts that you heard me talk about. Do this by yourself." Once time has expired, I then proceed to flip the hourglass again and ask that they turn to the student on their right and share their answers. Both students are checking on the other's information to see if they have left out any important facts. This is the part I enjoy the most. As I walk around, I listen to the discussion—there is a buzz like a swarm of bees. Afterward, we return to direct instruction and I ask them to take their notes in a traditional style. This time I review the essential question and ask that they listen and look for the answers. After five or so slides, I will do another three-minute drill.

This practice addresses the Common Core, and, as you can see, does not necessitate a complete overhaul of a teacher's instructional tool box. The sound practices Mr. Burke employs in his classroom already satisfy many facets of the Common Core. However, educators must scrutinize their practice to ensure their planned activities promote skill acquisition, upgrading the existing curriculum so that it becomes a vehicle for such practices. Modifying lessons so they focus on students' skills, rather than just content—this is where the hard work for educators lies!

Mr. Burke is successful in marrying the content (information about the conditions giving rise to the Industrial Revolution) to students' academic skill set. Let's break down his lesson and examine its instructional integrity in terms of the connection to the Common Core.

Teachers often struggle with students' attention span and, consequentially, their productivity. A rule of thumb: Consider the students' age, and then add or subtract two minutes (Jensen, 1995, p. 56). Considering that this example takes place in a tenth-grade classroom, the segments of each lesson (or as I refer to them, "instructional chunks") should be 12 minutes or shorter. By diversifying instruction in such a fashion, Mr. Burke delivers information through a variety of strategies, maintaining the attention of his class. The idea of breaking a lesson into instructional chunks is an integral element of sound instruction, student productivity, and lessons connected with the Common Core. You can see how the literacy piece fits in with the informational piece of a lesson that is constructed this way. The fact that the students are talking and writing reinforces their learning.

Mr. Burke begins with what Dr. Ray Heitzmann, professor of education at Villanova University, refers to as a "lecturette" to establish foundational knowledge.

As students follow his notes on the electronic white board, they are performing tasks specified by the Common Core Anchor Standards for Reading; as they read, they hone in on key ideas and details, tracking themes and ideas from the brief teacher-centered activity (Reading Standards 2, 3).

After two to three minutes, Mr. Burke stops his lecturette and asks students to formulate an essential question that will guide the lesson. Eliciting such information accesses the craft and structure (Reading Standard 5), where students are asked to analyze how details contribute to each other and to the overall meaning of the work studied. Students prove their understanding through this collaborative process, allowing Mr. Burke to informally assess the students' understanding as the lesson progresses. Eventually, Mr. Burke returns to another brief lecturette, incorporating charts, graphs and visual information for students to decipher. In doing so, students are integrating knowledge and ideas from the material (Reading Standard 7). This component of the lesson segues the students' movement to the cooperative-learning "chunk" of the lesson.

A series of studies explores active memory and cognitive function in a classroom setting. Research on the M Capacity, defined as the number of mental representations that one can keep activated in the working memory, shows that there is only so much information a student can internalize at one time (Pascual-Leone & Baillargeon, 1994, pp. 161–200). Therefore, asking students to pause, process information, and unload what they have learned before it "gets away" is a crucial component of a lesson. Mr. Burke makes use of this stop-and-jot method in his lesson. His students document their own interpretations of the essential question and expand upon what they hear and see throughout the teacher-centered portion of the lesson. By giving students the opportunity to demonstrate their knowledge of writing, this activity addresses the Common Core State Standards for Writing (Standard 2). As discussed earlier, it also provides Mr. Burke with another means of assessing student understanding.

Finally, as students share their ideas and compare and contrast their respective documentation, they are addressing Speaking and Listening Standards 2 and 4. The "buzz" is the flurry of discussion among the students, with Mr. Burke guiding them along as they create their own knowledge (Grubb, 1999, 32). This portion of the drill promotes content-specific vocabulary acquisition and use, a specific facet of the anchor standards for Language Standard 6.

The example you just read is a simple 10-minute component of a 41-minute lesson. Mr. Burke has employed this instructional strategy for a number of years, well before the advent of the Common Core, but look at everything that successfully pertains to the Common Core State Standards.

Put Your Thinking Cap on in English Class With Think Card

Mrs. Stephanie Piraino is a high school English teacher. She is well respected by her colleagues for her innovative and creative lessons and assessments. She makes use of an instructional tool she refers to as the Think Card to further engage students and facilitate the process of active reading.

This document, issued to students to complete as they read chapters of a literary piece, is essentially what I refer to as a "skeletal notes" tool. It provides students with a pathway to stop and jot as they read. She employs the Think Card because it is a fantastic means to inculcate literacy skills in her students, forcing them to ask questions and analyze text, make connections, and draw conclusions from the literature in her English curriculum.

Take a look at Mrs. Piraino's Think Card on the right. We will then briefly look at its connection to the CCSS.

THINK Card!

Active readers model certain behaviors every time they come in contact with a given text. As you read, THINK… it will help you to build a solid basis for deeper analysis. Use a think card for each chapter you read.

Thoughts: *What are your* **thoughts** *while reading the selection?*

How: **How** *do the conflicts in the selection drive the overall plot?*

Interpret: *Identify and* **interpret** *key quotes that assist in the progression of the selection.*

Need: *How are the characters in the selection driven by their* **needs**?

Know: *What do you* **know** *about the emerging themes and symbols after reading this section?*

Mrs. Piraino's chapter Think Card is simple in its construct and easy to implement as part of an instructional tool kit. Most importantly, it emphasizes elements of literacy stressed in the Common Core State Standards. It allows students to make routine use of the writing process and support and enrich their claims by gathering information to form an argument about the text (Writing Anchor Standards 1, 5, 8, 10). Also, the Think Card facilitates the process of reading closely and purposefully—all characteristics of active reading! In doing so, students are analyzing details of character and plot development and making interpretations about how each contributes to the overall meaning of the text (Reading Anchor Standards 1, 2, 4, 5, 10).

As I (Michael) have noted, teachers who make use of creative and engaging instructional methods should not fret when it comes to the implementation of the Common Core State Standards. Many of the incredible tools used in classrooms around the nation will successfully meet CCSS criteria. When looking at your own instruction, think about the engagement of students during your lessons. Think about the number of instructional modalities you use within a period or during an instructional block. And, most importantly, think about how the content you teach can be used as vehicle to practice literacy skills; such a change in mindset might be the spark needed to help you more easily mold your pedagogy to the Common Core.

The R.E.A.D. Strategy: Helping Students Tackle Multiple-Choice Questions

- **R**ead and Review
- **E**liminate
- **A**nalyze
- **D**ecide

Mr. Justin Cobis is a fifth-year social studies teacher, primarily working with ninth-grade students teaching the New York State global history and geography curriculum. Below is his story regarding assessing students and teaching test-taking skills.

After my first year teaching, I noticed that many of my students lacked basic skills in test taking. During my second year, I was teaching ESL/ELL (English as a Second Language/English Language Learners) and special education students in a collaborative setting. Again, both my co-teachers and I saw deficiencies in how our students dealt with the process of assessment, particularly multiple-choice questions. As part of our daily instructional routine, students were copying down and answering one multiple-choice question at the beginning of class. This "Do Now" activity helped established continuity and allowed for information to be introduced or reviewed while simultaneously presenting a daily time period to practice test-taking skills. By October, students were doing well copying down the question and doing their best at answering, but many seemed lost in finding the correct answer or even comprehending the meaning or objective of the question. This led me to create a formula for the students to use on any multiple-choice question, no matter the topic or subject.

The R.E.A.D. strategy is a four-step process to eliminate wrong choices in a multiple-choice question.

Step One: Read & Review. Students are to read the question and analyze it by underlining any key words or terms. The rationale behind this step is that students are actively engaged in looking for meaningful words and not discouraged if there are one or two words that they may not understand in the question.

Step Two: Eliminate. Students eliminate at least one, if not two choices from the question. While it may seem like common sense, I found that most of my students were rushing through questions without eliminating any answers first. If done correctly, this step allows for them to at least have a fifty-fifty chance at the correct answer. Multiple-choice questions are usually constructed so that at least one choice, maybe two, are fairly easy to spot as definitely wrong.

Step Three: Analyze. With only two or three choices remaining, the next step in the R.E.A.D. strategy involves analyzing the remaining choices. Students must revisit key words or terms highlighted in step one and think critically about the remaining choices.

Step Four: Decide. The final step is to have confidence and make a decision based on the process taken in steps one, two and three.

Putting it all together, the following is an example of what any one of my student's exam questions may look like after using the R.E.A.D. strategy. Note that I actually have them physically write out READ next to each question and check off each process.

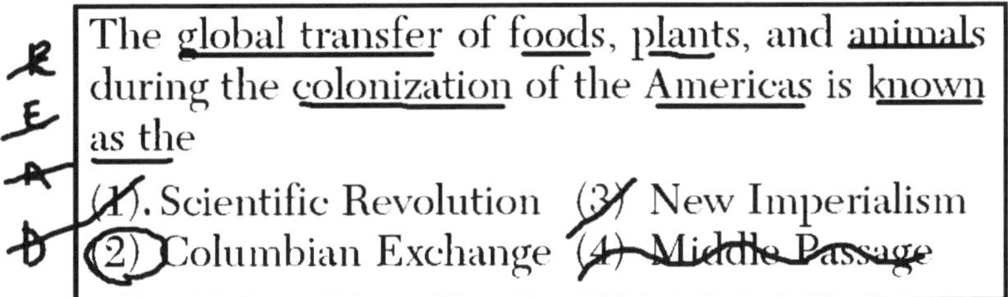

R
E
A
D

The global transfer of foods, plants, and animals during the colonization of the Americas is known as the

(1). Scientific Revolution (3) New Imperialism
(2) Columbian Exchange (4) Middle Passage

After several months, my students accepted this test-taking strategy and had new confidence in attacking multiple-choice questions. While the process of elimination has been around since the advent of multiple-choice exams, I have found that the R.E.A.D. acronym breaks down the process into simple stages. Since introducing the R.E.A.D. strategy in my collaborative and ESL/ELL classes, I have worked it into my ninth-grade world history AP classes. I believe that no matter the level of the students' mastery of a subject, or their test-taking skills in general, all students have something to gain from practicing the R.E.A.D. strategy.

Testing can be a tremendously stressful exercise for students (as well as parents, teachers, and administrators). This is often due to the historically troubled relationship between a) what is covered on the examination, b) the strategies (if any) students use to prepare for the exam, and c) the techniques students use while they take the exam. Testing in schools, however, will continue to be a mainstay as it is an efficient and objective measure of student performance. Authors Chickering and Schlossberg add:

> Tests can be significant opportunities for learning. They provide deadlines and contexts for assimilating and integrating prior learning. Thoughtful scrutiny of results yields information about gaps and confusions that can guide further learning. So our fundamental point about tests is to use them for learning opportunities, for consolidating prior preparation, for diagnosing purposes when the results are available. (1995, p. 183)

Although we might not usually look at it this way, the primary purpose of test-taking strategies is to improve student performance on examinations. A second but related purpose is to reduce exam anxiety. Making use of Mr. Cobis's R.E.A.D. strategy achieves both of these goals. As briefly mentioned above, and a point most poignant and applicable to this discussion, "When you take a test—any test—you're really being tested on two things: how much you know about the subject and how much you know about taking a test" (Kessleman-Turkel and Peterson, 1981, p. v). This is a critical skill teachers must teach, adding test-taking mastery to the students' proverbial toolbox of academic and even professional skills (many professions do require a written test for licensing, relicensing, and advancement). Knowing content is not enough! Students must be able to work through difficult assessments and understand what the questions are asking and know the appropriate way to answer. This is how students can truly perform well on any type of test! Understanding this, let's focus on the merits of Mr. Cobis's R.E.A.D. strategy and how it utilizes and strengthens literacy skills to improve student test performance.

The R.E.A.D. strategy provides students with skills to negotiate the often confusing multiple choice assessment. The higher-order thinking skills are analysis and evaluation. This systematic plan of attack allows students to deconstruct and analyze the detail of each question. These literacy skills are delineated in the Common Core State Standards for Reading (4–6 & 10). Because multiple-choice questions are often preceded by lengthy readings from primary and secondary source documents, students must develop the skills to compare information, assess point of view and critically read through complex text. Mr. Cobis's R.E.A.D. approach provides the platform for students to decipher content-specific vocabulary and phrases, understand how noncontent-specific words can steer the objective of each question, negotiate nuance within the question, and eliminate erroneous choices to come to the correct answer (Language Standards 4–6).

Mr. Cobis makes use of literacy skills found in the Common Core State Standards to work on test-taking skill. This "Do Now" instructional chunk, lasting less than five minutes, is an excellent strategy that, when used daily, allows for existing lesson and unit plans to seamlessly transition to meet the requirements of the Common Core while reinforcing content knowledge.

Reading and Writing to Learn in Science

Sean Bugara and Gary Delcioppo both teach seventh-grade life science. Each in his own way, Sean and Gary are perfect examples of teachers who use literacy activities in class to support science instruction, meeting the Common Core expectations for using literacy skills as a vehicle for having students process content.

I (Amy) visited Mr. Bugara's class on a day when they were clarifying and adding to information about the digestive process. The students got to work immediately, following Mr. Bugara's directions to list all the science words they could think of related to the digestive process. The students worked individually for a minute or so, after which Mr. Bugara and the class arranged the words into a graphic organizer, a step-by-step process of digestion. Because Mr. Bugara is very affirming to the students, and he had just given them a chance to briefly write down what they knew, their responses were generous and confident. He made etymological connections. For example, if we know that the stem *-gest* in *digestion* means "to carry," we can better understand other biological terms such as *egestion, ingest,* and *gestation.*

The graphic organizer depicted the organs comprising the alimentary canal, and some students asked, "What about the pancreas?" and "What about the liver?" Mr. Bugara explained that while organs like the esophagus and the stomach are "on the field," the pancreas, liver, and bile ducts are "on the bench." They are supportive players, contributing to the game when called upon. Mr. Bugara used this metaphor and others several times during the lesson. Creating the graphic organizer to label and explain the parts of the digestive system took about 12 minutes.

Next, the students were given a mock-up of the upcoming test on the digestive process. The questions on this test were similar in form, content, and language to their unit test. The students worked together for about 10 minutes, and then Mr. Bugara instructed them to check their answers against their notes, handouts, and textbook while he assisted pairs of students who were having difficulty. The test consisted of the caliber of questions found on the New York State Regents Exam in Living Environment, which these students will take at the end of eighth grade. When they take this high-stakes test, they will be familiar with its format, content, and language. The language of the test is replete with generic academic vocabulary, such as *indicates, products, structures, accomplished, function, represents, regulate, increase, decrease, result, procedure, individual, disorder, reducing, percent, extent,* and *sequential.* These words appear in sentences that feature content-specific words about biology, such as *secretions, hydrochloric acid, dehydration, carbohydrates, proteins, reabsorption, salivary enzymes, esophagus,* and *pepsin.*

Mr. Bugara took a moment to encourage students to visit his website where he had posted additional diagrams and helpful information.

With the few minutes of classtime remaining, students worked on an ongoing task, the creation of fold-up flashcards. These student-made study devices consist of four parts: a biological term, its definition, a *simple* student-drawn picture, and a personal way to connect its meaning to something the student can remember, like a mnemonic device or a metaphor. It's called a fold-up flashcard because the student creates it by folding a piece of paper in half length-wise, and then cutting one side of it in half, cross-wise, so that the term and definition are concealed by the cues (the picture and the mnemonic or metaphor). On Mr. Bugara's learning blog on his website, two of his students wrote posts about their fold-up flashcards and how they felt about doing their first biology lab.

> **Student 1:** I prepared for the quiz by making folding flashcards of all the vocab. and studying them. I got a 32/30, so I was very successful with this method. I enjoyed the lab because I got to look at different kinds of things, like a water flea, through a $600 microscope. I practiced and learned a lot of microscope skills like how to look at things on high power. Yes, I could teach a sixth grader how to use a microscope.

> **Student 2:** For the quiz, I made all of the definitions into folding flash cards. My mom quizzed me on them, and it worked out well. I was very happy with my grade, and it really helped out my average. As for the lab, I enjoyed it very much. I learned a lot from it and had a lot of fun doing it.

So in Sean Bugara's seventh-grade life science class, literacy, academic-vocabulary development, test-taking skills, productive class participation, study skills, meaningful use of technology (classroom website and learning blog), nonverbal processing (fold-up flashcards), learning through metaphor, and direct instruction all co-exist in the service of learning a challenging curriculum that was actually targeted by the New York State Education Department for tenth-grade students. (The course extends over a two-year span from seventh to eighth grade.) You can see how the literacy standards of the Common Core take their place, not as an add-on but as an inherent part of the learning plan, in which students actively work with the concepts and terminology.

Gary Delcioppo, teaching the same course at the same level, centralizes literacy and language skills of the Common Core in the problem-solving discovery process of science. Mr. Delcioppo believes that in science class, the students have to think and communicate and figure things out based on principles and evidence. Then they have to express their conclusions in coherent, well-developed sentences.

In Mr. Delcioppo's class, students are divided into groups of three. His recipe is to blend one highly motivated student with one not-so-motivated student and with one student who will probably have a neutral effect on the group. Observe. Remix, as necessary.

After a limited amount of direct teaching, the students are expected to work together to solve problems presented to them in writing. The written information consists of both paragraphs and numerical information (charts, graphs, diagrams, tables, timelines, Venn diagrams, etc.). A small number of pages is assigned, interspersed with questions/problems that require complete written sentences as answers/solutions.

At frequent checkpoints, the students line up to meet briefly with Mr. Delcioppo, who either approves their work or sends them back to correct the form, procedure, or content. Students are expected to follow directions and to complete their work thoroughly. And they do!

In both Mr. Bugara's and Mr. Delcioppo's classes, the students are relaxed and confident, but purposeful and definitely serious about and engaged in learning biology.

Both Sean Bugara and Gary DelCioppo provide the students with everything they need to be successful, but they also give them the opportunity *in class* to construct meaning for themselves through peer-to-peer conversation and writing-to-learn expectations.

Part 2

Writing

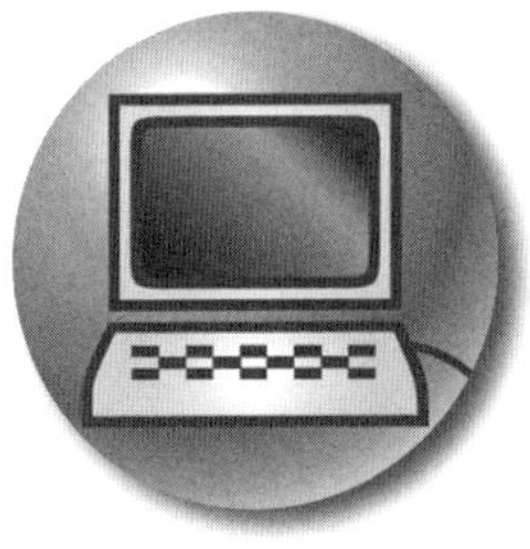

CHAPTER 4

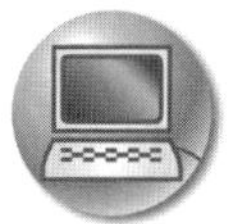

Writing and the Common Core

The writing standards center on three kinds of writing: argumentation, information, and narrative. The emphasis, however, is decidedly on argumentation, the ability to marshal evidence and convincingly present a well-considered case to a particular audience.

Teaching writing has multiple components: teaching students how to generate ideas; how to organize ideas into a unified, finished composition; how to use the conventions of grammar, spelling, punctuation, capitalization, and paragraphing; how to revise and then edit; and how to use formal and technical vocabulary. All of these components add up to one thing: *how to meet the reader's expectations*. Writing is a solitary activity, but it is informed by social interactions. It is easy to slip into a state of mind that focuses so intently on the act of writing that we actually forget about the reader.

Writing transmits information to a reader, but that is not its only function. Writing supports learning, whether there is a reader or not. Writing helps us shape, focus on, apply, and remember information and experience. We write ourselves into understanding. Therefore, not everything that students write needs to be read and evaluated by the teacher. Indeed, it can be said that if you read and evaluate everything your students write, they are not writing nearly enough. Students need to take original notes, compose lists, participate in blogs and other online communications, and engage in all kinds of informal, not-to-be-evaluated forms of writing. In fact, informal writing is a part of the Common Core State Standards for Writing.

Breaking Down the Standards

Below are simplified statements of the standards, followed by the original language (www.corestandards.org).

Types and Purposes

1. **Write arguments.** Write arguments to support claims in an analysis of substantive topics or texts, using valid reasoning and relevant and sufficient evidence.

2. **Write informative/explanatory texts.** Write informative/explanatory texts to examine and convey complex ideas and information clearly and accurately through the effective selection, organization, and analysis of content.

3. **Write narratives.** Write narratives to develop real or imagined experiences or events using effective techniques, well-chosen details, and well-structured event sequences.

   Note: In English language arts, teachers are expected to address these three types of writing explicitly and individually, building the skills students will apply to the other subject areas. In the other subject areas, students may be expected to blend the three types into a single writing piece. For example, an anecdote or two strengthens argumentation, as does the inclusion of information (such as data, cause-effect statements, embedded definitions, explanations).

Production and Distribution

4. **Match your style to the expectations of the audience.** Produce clear and coherent writing in which the development, organization, and style are appropriate to task, purpose, and audience.

5. **Use the writing process.** Develop and strengthen writing as needed by planning, revising, editing, rewriting, or trying a new approach.

6. **Use technology as a collaborative tool.** Use technology, including the Internet, to produce and publish writing and to interact and collaborate with others.

Research to Build and Present Knowledge

7. **Conduct short as well as more sustained research projects.** Conduct short as well as more sustained research projects based on focused questions, demonstrating understanding of the subject under investigation.

8. **Gather information from multiple sources.** Judge the accuracy of your sources. Use proper citations. Avoid plagiarism. Gather relevant information from multiple print and digital sources, assess the credibility and accuracy of each source, and integrate the information while avoiding plagiarism.

9. **Use both literary and informational texts to support, inform, and enrich your claims.** Draw evidence from literary or informational texts to support analysis, reflection, and research.

Range of Writing

10. **Write routinely; write *both* formally and informally, depending on the expectations of the audience; write polished pieces, revised over time; *also*, write on-demand pieces within a short time frame, such as a single class period; use writing as *both* a means for learning and a way to demonstrate your knowledge.** Write routinely over extended time frames (time for research, reflection, and revision) and shorter time frames (a single setting or a day or two) for a range of tasks, purposes, and audiences.

Regarding the range and content of the Writing Standards, the Common Core State Standards document (www.corestandards.org) says this:

> For students, writing is a key means of asserting and defending claims, showing what they know about a subject, and conveying what they have experienced, imagined, thought, and felt. To be college- and career-ready writers, students must take task, purpose, and audience into careful consideration, choosing words, information, structures, and formats deliberately. They need to know how to combine elements of different kinds of writing—for example, to use narrative strategies within argument and explanation within narrative—to produce complex and nuanced writing. They need to be able to use technology strategically when creating, refining, and collaborating on writing. They have to become adept at gathering information, evaluating sources, and citing material accurately, reporting findings from their research and analysis of sources in a clear and cogent manner. They must have the flexibility, concentration, and fluency to produce high-quality first-draft text under a tight deadline as well as the capacity to revisit and make improvements to a piece of writing over multiple drafts when circumstances encourage or require it. (p. 41)

In the next chapter, we will be talking about creating a culture of writing in the classroom, using writing as a tool for learning in science (with applicability to all subjects), writing a cogent argument, and incorporating sources in writing.

CHAPTER 5

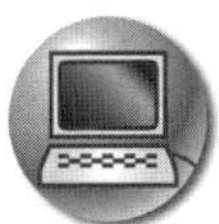

Creating a Writing Culture: What Do Students Need?

In their schooling, students engage in all kinds of writing, and the instructional implications vary depending on the audience, purpose, and genre. In the elementary grades, when students are just getting their sea legs, so to speak, as writers, they often describe or respond to personal experiences. They write about their family and friends, tell anecdotes, make up charming stories, and compose poetry in various forms.

Writers of prompt-based writing need the learning experiences listed in Figure 5.1, which all teachers, not just English teachers, can provide. By providing these learning experiences to support writing, the skills of writing work to strengthen knowledge of the content.

Figure 5.1. Learning Experiences That Support Writing

- Emulation
- Opportunities to use writing as a tool for learning
- Explicit instructions
- Feedback that will be *helpful*, not just critical
- Breakdown of research skills
- Instruction on how to integrate sources

- Pinpointing of potential problems and addressing them in advance
- Time and guidance provided during the revision and editing process

Emulation

We often hear "We learn to write by writing." Actually, we learn to write by *reading*. Not only does reading supply the information that writers need, reading also develops awareness of what writing is supposed to look like. Writing style is a special kind of language. Unlike speech, writing involves conventions such as spelling, punctuation, the creation of complete sentences (mostly declarative ones), and certain expressions and sentence structures heard rarely in speech but seen often in written text. Writing style is informed primarily by reading, but the gaps can be filled in by explicit instruction. Explicit instruction cannot make up for deficits in reading. When it comes to becoming a good writer, time spent reading is paramount, not time spent receiving explicit instruction, and certainly not time spent filling in single-answer worksheets. "(George) Hillocks (1986), after an extensive review … found that writing classes that emphasized free writing did not produce significantly better writing than comparison classes" (Krashen, 2004, p. 135).

The reason we can learn reading by reading but not writing by writing makes sense. Language is acquired "from input, not output, from comprehension, not production" (Krashen, 2004, p. 136). And the type of writing we learn to do from reading depends on the kind of reading that we do. If we want to learn to write five-paragraph essays, we should read a lot of them; if we want to learn to write a cogent argument, we should read editorials; if we want to learn to write personal narratives, we should read memoirs. Writing style is acquired through unconscious emulation of the vocabulary and phraseology of targeted genres, just as a person's speaking style is acquired through unconscious emulation of the speech that is poured into their ears. The strategy couldn't be simpler. *Have students read in the genres that you want them to learn to write.*

Opportunities to Use Writing as a Tool for Learning

To say, as we did earlier, that learning to write depends more on reading (within the targeted genre) than on writing alone is not to dismiss the value of writing as a means for understanding. If our students write regularly, their writing style will not improve (by writing alone), but frequent writing has other benefits, primarily that writing helps us find and untangle our own thoughts. This is writing to learn, and students need to do more of it. Writing allows for the extended conversation with the self that *in itself* generates answers and solutions that we knew but didn't know we knew. We write our way into knowing, just as we can sometimes answer our own questions and solve our own problems just by talking them through. Language itself generates thoughts.

> Perhaps the clearest experimental evidence showing that writing helps thinking is from a series of studies by Langer and Applebee (1987, in Krashen, 2004). High school students were asked to read social studies passages and then study the information in them either by writing an analytic essay on an assigned question relating to the passage, or by using other study techniques (e.g. note-taking, answering comprehension questions, writing summaries). Students were then given a variety of tests on the information in the passages. The results showed that any kind of written response leads to better performance than does reading without writing. In their third study, they showed that essay writing did not result in greater retention when the reading passage was easy; when the passage they read was difficult, however, essay writers did much better than students using other study techniques. (Krashen, 2004, p. 139)

Many teachers feel the pressure of time in addressing all of the required topics. This is especially true in social studies, science, and math. When a teacher uses language like "How am I supposed to get through my curriculum?" "I have to cover this, this, and this!" and "I'm so far behind where I'm supposed to be at this point in the year," we know that teacher needs help in balancing the quantity of learning with the quality of what is actually learned. To paraphrase Albert Einstein, learning is what is left over after we have forgotten everything we have been taught. To adhere slavishly to a curriculum calendar is to forego the teachable moments, to press on regardless of student curiosity, lack of comprehension, or the resulting lack of interest. To sacrifice skill development for relentless content dissemination is a losing proposition. Sure that the students can't or won't read and write to learn on their own, we watch as their skills stagnate and eventually atrophy. The less they read and write to make and remember meaning for themselves, the more we lecture—the more we lecture, the less they need to do, and the worse they get at independent learning.

Enter writing as a tool for learning, also called comprehension checks. A comprehension check is a break that turns passive learning into active learning via a writing-to-learn moment. The writing-to-learn moment focuses the student, allowing her to monitor her own understanding; it also provides diagnostic information (formative assessment) to the teacher. This information should direct instruction. When students work in pairs to produce their written responses, the likelihood of universal participation is increased. The strategy is to give simple prompts: *label a diagram, write one or two sentences, make a list, solve a problem, pose a relevant problem, write a possible test item, complete a sentence starter, make a Venn diagram, paraphrase.*

Explicit Instruction

Let's turn our attention to formal writing pieces. These are also tools for learning, but they are to be assessed against formal criteria. Because assigning is not teaching any more than shouting, "Now go out and win this game!" is coaching, we need to regard the crafting of a formal writing assignment as just that—a craft. As with any craft, we will discover the errors of our ways when we see the product, which is the student's writing piece. You spend a great deal of time reading and evaluating student writing; most teachers find it frustrating and tedious (with the possible exception of creative writing and personal narrative). While we don't claim the ability to throw pixie dust on a stack of student papers to endow them with charm and wisdom, we do have experience with crafting the instructions to elicit more focused information expressed in appropriate language.

Here is a well-crafted writing task that uses the three-part structure we are recommending.

1. Minerals have properties that can make them useful. Select a mineral and, in a well-developed paragraph, explain how and why its properties make it useful.
2. Recommended words from the Academic Word List (see p. 169): *transform, generate, phase, expand, category, capable, alternative, bond, precise*
3. Recommended sentence frames:
   - ____________________ is useful because ________________.
   - ____________________ is used for ______________ because of its ______________________________
   - Because ____________________ is ________________, it is used to ____________.

Now let's analyze the strength of this model. Part 1 cleanly defines the task in two sentences. The first sentence hands the student a general statement about the topic that she is welcome to lift, verbatim and without attribution, in her paragraph. Note that, since this is straight-up informational writing, we are not looking for a fancy "hook" to intrigue the reader. In a personal narrative, argument, or story, we would want the first sentence to have some come-hither appeal, but this is a "just-the-facts-ma'am" situation. The second sentence of Part 1 sets forth the two task verbs in no uncertain terms: *select* and *explain*. You might be surprised at how many teachers, and therefore students, are vague in their task verbs. "I want them to *respond* to …"; "I want them to *think deeply* about …"; I want them to *tell me* something about … ." Compare these unclear and unhelpful directives to task verbs like *analyze, compare, explain, select, illustrate, trace,* and *evaluate*. This sentence also specifies the expected length and form, *a well-developed* paragraph.

If we were to stop right there, we would be simulating the kind of task directive that students might find on a high-stakes assessment. However, since this writing piece is to be a *learning* experience as well as an assessment tool, we include two scaffolding devices: generic academic vocabulary and sentence-structure frames.

For the generic academic-vocabulary scaffold, we want just a handful of words that will work well in this task. We're looking for those Tier II words that the student probably knows but would not have used without prompting. The student is not expected to use all of them, just those that work well naturally and elevate the language tone. Keep in mind that we're going for Tier II generic academic words rather than Tier III, words found in the glossary. This is because the Tier III words come naturally when writing about a domain-specific topic, but the Tier II words may not. The student would probably use Tier III words like *gypsum, cleavage, crystal,* and *granule* in a report about minerals; she might not use the generic words we've suggested. It is those generic words that properly contextualize the Tier III words, like a gem set in a gold setting instead of embedded in clay.

The second scaffold, the sentence frames, helps the student write at least one clean, clear sentence. If properly done, the sentence frame can be used for other writing pieces. The sentence frame differs from a fill-in-the-blank structure in that it is without specific content. A sentence like "Because ________ is a soft and flaky mineral, it is used to make powder for cosmetics" would be a fill-in-the-blank, not a generic sentence frame that can be reused for another writing task. In other words, the sentence frame is a generic template, in this case, for informational writing. If we wanted, for example, a description of a mineral that included its properties and uses, a helpful sentence might look something like this:

> ______________ is a mineral used for ____________________
> because of its ___________________________________.

The student would be expected to go on from here to be more specific about the properties and how they make the mineral useful.

Breaking Down the Skills of Research

The Common Core recommends multiple shorter research pieces, spaced throughout the school year, rather than the one monster term paper of the past. Any kind of research paper involves the pursuit, evaluation, organization, presentation, and attribution of sources. All a research paper involves, when all is said and done, is answering a question by finding out more than you knew to begin with, deciding what to leave in and what to leave out of your answer, writing the answer coherently, and giving credit to those who wrote things whose writings assisted you.

A model for a research project that is actually student friendly is called the I-Search, developed by Ken Macrorie (1988). An I-Search integrates formal research with a narrative of the student's journey to find the answer or to broaden his knowledge about something he is interested in. In the I-Search format, students frame their own question and then go about searching for information to answer it, eventually formulating a coherent answer in writing. However, the I-Search is introduced by the student's narrative about why this question interests him. It also includes a narrative about how he went about doing the search itself. He presents the information, citing sources in proper and age-appropriate format, and then concludes with a narrative of what he learned about the topic itself and about doing the I-Search project.

I (Amy) suspect that the reason for problems like procrastination, plagiarism, and incoherence that teachers encounter with traditional research papers has to do with students' distance from the project. Feeling that the research paper genre is formal and academic, students don't commit to it. What they are writing about doesn't matter to them. What matters is "sounding smart." That surely is the best way to produce the worst kind of writing. But the I-Search is a nice transition in the later elementary and middle school years from the personal narratives that students "live inside" to the research paper, which is objective and spoken from a voice that needs to sound "outside" the writer. The personal-narrative element of the I-Search acts as a scaffold, allowing the student to maintain his voice and explore personal interests while reporting on information supported by research.

The following is a description of an I-Search unit created by Make It Happen! (www2.edc.org/fsc/mih/i-search.html)

I-Search Unit

The I-Search unit is the very heart of Make It Happen! because it links effective teaching, learning (content knowledge and research processes), and assessment. Based on Ken Macrorie's 1988 book *The I-Search Paper,* the Education Development Center (EDC) has developed an I-Search unit with four phases of instruction.

In **Phase I**, teachers immerse students in the unit's theme (i.e., a socially relevant topic that naturally links science, social studies, language arts, and mathematics). Students engage in a variety of activities, not only to discover what they already know about this theme but also to build background knowledge. These activities model a variety of ways for students to gather information. By the end of Phase I, each student poses an I-Search question to guide his or her personally motivated inquiry.

In **Phase II**, students develop a search plan that identifies how they will gather information: by reading books, magazines, newspapers, reference materials; by watching videos or filmstrips; by interviewing people or conducting surveys; by carrying out experiments, doing simulations, or going on field trips.

In **Phase III**, students follow their search plans and gather information. They also analyze and synthesize information to construct knowledge.

In **Phase IV**, students draft, revise, edit, and publish an I-Search report. The I-Search Report includes the following components: **My Search Questions**, **My Search Process**, **What I Learned**, **What This Means To Me**, and **References**. The report becomes the foundation for an oral presentation, skit, poster, experiment, or other display of knowledge.

An I-Search unit is an excellent context for alternative assessment, the inclusion of students with diverse learning abilities, and **technology integration**.

The skills that are synthesized to complete a research project are as follows:

1. The skill of narrowing a unit of study into a question or task
2. The skill of searching for information
3. The skill of determining if the information is valid, relevant, appropriate, and contributory

4. The skill of managing the information: keeping track of sources, filing and labeling, note taking, ordering
5. The skill of making an outline to organize and generate main ideas and details. This involves analyzing and synthesizing information from various sources, deciding what to use and what to discard, and deciding what to quote directly and what to paraphrase.
6. The skill of converting the outline into a coherent report, organized around paragraphs, each paragraph having a topic sentence
7. The skill of integrating and citing direct quotations and paraphrases of information found in sources
8. The skill of creating a Works Cited page according to a style guide, such as MLA
9. The skill of converting a rough draft into a final draft by revising and editing

Instruction in How to Integrate Resources

The writer has many choices for integrating information taken from sources: direct quotes that fit within the paragraph, block quotes, paraphrases, charts and graphs, links to websites, and links to podcasts and videos (if the report is intended to be read online).

The concept and practice of integrating sources into one's own writing is difficult to master and takes a long time and patient, well-sequenced instruction. Effective instruction is usually lacking, as evidenced by the results. We make a lot of assumptions about what *should* have already been taught and learned at a given grade level or by a different teacher. While the English teacher is teaching how to deconstruct Mark Antony's soliloquy, the social studies teacher is expecting that the students are good to go on MLA citations of primary sources. To students, citing sources is an arcane, tedious, confusing, and seemingly unnecessary detail. You can't blame them for forgetting if the commas go inside or outside the quotation marks and if it's the author's last name or the year of publication that goes inside the parentheses. The language of citation is unfamiliar: *in-text citation, direct quotation, indirect quotation, parenthetical citation, attribution, running acknowledgement, etc.* There's not going to be a lot of retention, so if you want accuracy in attribution, you're going to find yourself teaching it—yes, even though it's been taught before, and, yes, even though it will have to be taught again after you.

Fortunately, teaching integration of sources in your subject area does not have to be onerous. In accordance with the philosophy of teaching writing through models, you'll need to find models of the kind of writing you're looking for and then engage students in a little inductive reasoning. *What do you notice? Are there quotation marks? Why? What words are capitalized in the quotation? What happens at the end of the quotation? How does the author introduce the quotation? Why are there sometimes no quotation marks around someone's direct words?*

In other words, rather than saying, "here are the rules," engage students in authentic models and have them observe, report, and draw conclusions.

Providing Time and Guidance During the Revision and Editing Process

Most students need frequent in-class checkpoints and instruction during the writing process of constructing a research paper. Rather than frontloading the instruction, deliver relevant instruction during the process at the point of need. If you instruct students on skills too early, they are never going to remember how to cite their sources, use transitional words, write a conclusion, or rework their introduction to have it forecast what the paper actually says.

Feedback That Is Helpful, Not Just Critical

Listen to an eighth-grader learning to practice the clarinet, and you'll hear all kinds of squeaks and squawks that only a mother could love. While we wouldn't think of judging the fledgling musician, athlete, or chef against the standards we'd use for professionals, we somehow think we are obligated to be merciless when it comes to the growing pains of young writers.

No one can fix everything all at once. Writing is a sophisticated skill that takes years of reading, writing, and instruction to master. The writing skills of a group of students will vary widely. The writing performance of a single student will also vary widely, depending on the topic and the audience.

There is no Order of the Red Pen knighthood to be bestowed upon teachers who catch every punctuation slipup on student papers. No luncheons are held in honor of the teacher who has had the sharpest eye for misspellings. Our job is to encourage and instruct students on their journeys toward becoming acceptable writers for college and career readiness. (Creative writing is a joyful and fruitful pursuit, but there's a reason why the Common Core wants us to lean toward informational and argumentative writing). If you were learning a new and complex skill, you wouldn't want to be bombarded with "feedback" on every little transgression. You'd want 1) encouragement on what you were doing right and 2) some specific corrective advice that you could apply next time.

When it comes to giving feedback on student writing, the use of rubrics is helpful because rubrics give the students an at-a-glance look at overall expectations. Rubrics allow students to track their progress and to know the criteria in advance of writing.

Rubrics can and should be simple. Before the word *rubric* came to be used in education, I devised a little strip of paper that I (Amy) affixed to my students' writing. It looked like this:

Addressing the question____________
Development (reasons, examples, specifics)__________
Vocabulary/Sentence Style__________________
Organization__________________________
Grammar, Spelling, Punctuation, Capitalization__________________
Other____

I did not feel obligated to correct every infraction on the paper. Nor did I feel obligated to comment on each of these categories. If my students knew 1) the components of a writing task, 2) what they were doing well, and 3) what they could work on next time, I felt that was appropriate feedback.

But I did one more thing, and it's the thing most rarely done with student writing. I directed the students to a website I had designed (www.henhudschools.org/uploads/rxwrite/home.htm) that provided the additional work that *they* needed to do to improve. You can correct apostrophes and make marginal comments (*Be specific!*) all day long, but as long as the working end of the stick remains in your hand, and not in the hands of the students, they will continue to look at the grade and not the corrections, and they will continue to make the same mistakes. With RxWrite, a collection of differentiated online mini-lessons, improvement is in the student's hands.

In summary, a simple rubric works best, coupled with limited but helpful positive and negative feedback, plus some mechanism for having students follow up to correct their mistakes and/or learn how to develop their ideas so that they move toward continuous improvement.

Finally, Practice!

Finally, although writing is developed primarily through reading, students need regular practice writing in every subject (not just English class). The crafting of a single meaningful sentence that employs academic vocabulary and is done as part of class can be just as valuable, or more so, than a report that is assigned but not taught. A science teacher can toss out a few generic academic words and ask for a one-sentence summary of yesterday's lesson on rock formation. A social studies teacher can ask for a list of words and phrases related to Marbury v. Madison. An art teacher can ask for a definition in the student's own words of any number of art-related terms. As students read aloud their sentences, everyone benefits by hearing not only the information, but also the sentence forms because written English sounds different from spoken English.

CHAPTER 6

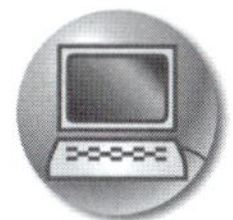

Writing to Learn: Science, Meet Syntax. Syntax, This Is Science.

I often hear content area teachers say, "I don't care if they write in complete sentences, just as long as they give me the information." Teachers who say this probably mean that they don't want students in a science or social studies class "getting bogged down" in rules about complete sentences, punctuation, spelling, and capitalization. These teachers may be overlooking the learning opportunity of having students learn *through* writing complete substantial sentences. A sentence, after all, expresses a relationship, the relationship between something or someone (the subject) and what that subject is, has, or does (the predicate). Writing a particular type of sentence in accordance with instructions is more than just adherence to conventions: it's actually a powerful way to construct, remember, and apply knowledge.

We'll look first at the kinds of complete-sentence writing that is probably *not* particularly instructive in itself. Sometimes, the answer to a question can be jotted down in a single word or phrase, but let's look at what happens when we accept shortcuts for the sake of convenience:

1. Q: Name the three states of matter.
A: solid, liquid, gas

This answer is acceptable because the question is so low level. To have the student write out "The three states of matter are solid, liquid, and gas" would be to adhere to a rule for its own sake, not for the sake of clarity or completeness.

2. Q: What is a mixture?
A: two or more substances blended together

This answer is more problematical. Although the answer is correct, we don't know from it whether the student understands the difference between a mixture and a compound. What do the words "blended together" really mean in a scientific context?

3. Q: Explain the difference between a heterogeneous mixture and a homogeneous mixture and give an example of each.
A: Heterogeneous = unevenly mixed, beach sand
Homogeneous = evenly mixed, sugar and water

This answer is insufficient. In being so abbreviated, it lacks respect for the reader (the teacher), putting the onus on you to determine whether the student knows the information or not. But this is what we inevitably get whenever we settle for a written responses that is just a word a two.

The models that follow use simple grammatical concepts to help students organize and create relationships among facts. You don't have to be an English teacher or a grammar wiz to explain the sentence models. You just have to use the templates, as explained below. It takes a very short amount of class time to demonstrate how they are used.

Let's say that a science teacher, whom we'll call Mrs. L, has taught a lesson series about types of matter. The key points:

- Any substance having mass and volume is matter.
- The elements that form matter determine its characteristics.
- Any substance that cannot be further broken down is an element. Elements are comprised of only one kind of atom. Each element is represented by its own chemical symbol on a chart known as the periodic table.
- Atoms bond to form compounds and molecules. These are represented by chemical formulas.
- A mixture is the result of the blending of two or more substances.
- Heterogeneous mixtures consist of an uneven blend of two or more substances. The distinct parts of a heterogeneous mixture can actually be seen.
- Homogeneous mixtures consist of an even blend of two substances such that we cannot distinguish them visually.

Language-wise, what we have here are several terms that the students might be familiar with in ordinary conversation (*matter, mixture, bond*) or academic conversations (*elements, substance, symbol, mass, volume*), as well as a few science-only words (*heterogeneous, homogeneous, chemical, atom, molecule*). Students need to learn to narrow their mental definitions of these words to fit a specific scientific context. If they also can connect the science-specific definition to the definition that they already know, they will grasp the concept on a fuller level than if they think they have to abandon prior understandings in order to accommodate the science-specific meaning.

But we also have lots of concepts that can be related to each other if we know how to construct sentences that are capable of showing relationships. Let's look at how giving students templates for four kinds of sentences can deepen their understanding of the concepts and help them remember the language.

Please don't be daunted by grammatical terminology. We want you to present these templates to students in the simplest way possible. If you think the term "coordinating conjunction" or "appositive" will cause an immediate shutdown, just use metaphors like "hitching device" for coordinating conjunction and "another way to name it" for appositive.

Understanding Science by Compound Sentences

Compound sentences are two or more complete sentences that the writer has decided to marry by means of a coordinating conjunction. For Mrs. L's purposes, the coordinating conjunctions are *and* (to express relationships that are cumulative, *but* (to express relationships that are contrastive), and *so* (to express relationships that are contrastive or causal).

Her writing-to-learn-science lesson is given as a review before the unit test. She gives the students key words and instructs them to compose a sentence using either *and*, *but*, or *so* to express a relationship. The students work together and then read their sentences aloud to the class. Here is what the activity might look like.

Key words: chemical symbol, chemical formula

- Sentences: A *chemical symbol* on the periodic table represents each element, and when the atoms bond into molecules, the molecules are represented by a *chemical formula*.
- A *chemical symbol* represents an atom of an element, but a *chemical formula* represents a molecule.

Students have to work together, talking about not only the meaning of the individual terms, but about how they are related to each other, and how to express that in a well-constructed sentence. This task is much more advanced than simply asking students to use a word in a sentence, an exercise that is not challenging or illuminating and does not require communication between students.

Understanding Science by Appositives

You read appositives all the time. An appositive is simply a phrase that specifies what comes before it. An appositive is set off by commas.

- The three primary colors of light, *red, blue, and green*, produce white light when added together.
- Torque, *the force that rotation causes*, is equal to the product of the force times the distance to the axis of rotation.

Note that appositives may also be expressed parenthetically. It's the writer's choice.

Appositives are useful and important to know for reading comprehension as well as for writing. We can assess a student's knowledge of a term by asking for sentences using appositives. Students can paraphrase information by writing sentences using appositives.

Understanding Science by Semicolons

Let's review semicolons. There are two uses of semicolons, and we'll address how both can help students process information through reading and writing.

The more common of the two uses of semicolons is simply to connect closely related independent clauses, groups of words that could stand alone as sentences. (Catch the appositive?) Why not just leave well enough alone, keeping the two independent clauses as separate sentences? Well, if ideas are very closely related, we want the reader to keep them together. Keeping such closely related ideas together actually improves comprehension (assuming that the reader knows what a semicolon signals). Why not just combine the independent clauses by creating a compound sentence with a comma and coordinating conjunction, namely *and*? Well, you could. A semicolon is not better than the comma-*and* construction. But you might already have more than one *and* elsewhere in the sentence, joining parts within the sentence like two or more nouns, verbs, or modifiers. Too many *ands* and the reader gets confused between big chunks and smaller chunks within the sentence. So here are two examples of semicolons joining closely related independent clauses:

- In any collision, momentum is conserved; energy, similarly, is also conserved.

Note how this sentence could also have been written with a compound subject (...*momentum and energy are conserved*...). That would be fine as well, but it could be argued that separating *momentum* and *energy* into their own clauses helps the reader to notice, and therefore process, each concept individually.

- A collision in which the colliding objects are greatly affected is called an inelastic collision; a collision in which the colliding objects just bounce off each other is called an elastic collision.

Note how the two clauses of this sentence are written in the same grammatical form. We call this technique parallel structure. Parallel structure facilitates comprehension of like concepts.

The second application for semicolons is used less often. We use a semicolon to separate items in a series when the items themselves contain commas. The reason for the semicolon is to help the reader separate the items. Below, we've combined this use of a semicolon in a sentence having appositives:

- Momentum can be played with for human amusement. Examples of this include Newton's Cradle, a device that mesmerizes you with its rhythmic bouncing steel balls; a roller coaster, a thrill based on energy conservation; and bumper cars, whose fun results from collision.

The series application of semicolons is a great way to have students think of examples and explain them in a single well-controlled sentence.

Understanding Science by Colons

Everyone knows that a colon may be used after *as follows* or *the following* at the end of a sentence. That's a great starting point. Students can be instructed to use a colon to introduce a list of examples. A colon is also used to explain, or to state something more plainly, as follows:

- The test was unreliable: when we replicated the experiment, the results were inconsistent.

A colon may also be used to emphasize a point about to be made. It is effective to use a number in this kind of sentence:

- Our experiment failed for one reason: our research methods were unsound.
- There are three things to do when you car starts to smoke: pull over immediately, distance yourself from the car, and call for assistance.

The writing-to-learn techniques described above result in thoughtful processing of information. That is their value, the reason to take time in a science or any other content-based class to engage them. It is not expected that the science teacher will actually teach the sentence forms. That is the job of the English teacher. So if the English department has not taught the sentence forms, science cannot meet syntax in the service of science. On the other hand, if the English teacher is the only one in whose class students apply what they know about sentence forms (syntax), students will not get enough practice to leverage their content knowledge with their writing abilities. Both subjects lose out unless there is coordination.

CHAPTER 7

Writing a Cogent Argument

Of the three text types that the Common Core specifies (informational, argumentation, narrative), it is argumentation that is considered most important. At the elementary level, 30 percent of the writing that students do should express an opinion and give reasons for it. At the middle school level, that proportion rises to 35 percent, and the content is elevated to supporting an argument with evidence. And at the high school level, 40 percent of the writing that students do should support an argument with evidence. The Common Core defines argument as that which "includes the ability to analyze and assess our facts with evidence, support our solutions, and defend our interpretations and recommendations with clarity and precision in every subject area" (www.engageny.org). Writing an argument is more than evidence of learning. The process of using higher-order thinking skills (analysis, synthesis, evaluation) to assemble an argument from relevant, reliable facts and anecdotes "dramatically increases our ability to retain, retrieve, apply, and synthesize knowledge" (www.engageny.org).

Let's clarify the difference between the terms *persuasive essay* and *argumentation*. Although both forms seek to influence an audience, argumentation is based more on evidence and logic, while persuasion is based more on emotional appeals. Argumentation is more objective, and hence more intellectually rigorous. If a student were asked to persuade her parents to let her get a four-legged pet, she might resort to whatever works between her and her parents: whining, pouting, insisting, and threatening to run away would be fair game, assuming such techniques have worked in the past. If she were asked to create an argument for why she should have a four-legged pet, and if the audience were less subjective than her parents—let's say, the directors of an animal shelter—she should offer evidence about her suitability as a potential pet owner: her history taking care of someone or something that depended on her, her knowledge, her schedule, her physical strength. The Common Core definitely seeks to wean students from emotional responses and transition them into more substantial reasoning.

So how can we get students to become skillful writers of argumentation? As with any form of writing, the best teacher is the reader's eye. Social studies teachers already use seminal historical documents that set forth arguments. Science teachers can use articles in accessible magazines and newspapers. Teachers in the arts can use reviews. English language arts teachers can use interesting, well-written editorials. (Figure 7.1 lists questions and tasks to use with editorials.) Through these models, we can help students understand how argumentation works and what the writer had to know and do to produce them.

Figure 7.1. Essential Questions and Tasks for Analyzing Editorials

About the Issue

1. What is the issue?
2. Why is the issue important?
3. Why is the issue controversial?

About the Argument and Techniques

1. **Driving the point home through repetition.** In an editorial, the author usually states his or her main point (opinion) several times. Look at the editorial and highlight the sentences or questions in it that state the author's main point (opinion).
2. **Stats.** Circle any statistics that you find in the editorial.
3. **Stories to prove the point.** There may be anecdotes (little stories about people) in the editorial. If you find one, place either a smiley face or sad face over it.
4. **Street creds.** Is the author notable? If so, what are his or her credentials for writing the editorial? What, if anything, makes you believe that this author is an expert on the subject?
5. **Cause-effect.** All arguments rest on implicit or explicit cause-and-effect relationships. (However, not all purported cause-and-effect relationships are necessarily valid. A common logical fallacy is to

attribute correlation to causality, and readers should learn to look for this. Look for the words *if* and *then* to find explicit cause-effect statements. Also, look for words such as *so, because, thus, therefore,* and *that is why*.)

6. **Diction.** Look for words that have positive or negative connotations. Underline these and write *P* or *N* in the margin. (For example: The words *professional photographers of celebrities* and *paparazzi* may refer to the same people, but *professional photographers of celebrities* has a positive connotation while *paparazzi* has a negative one.)

Every year, students should read at least ten editorials or opinion pieces in every class and analyze them before writing their own. If this sounds like a lot, the amount is justified for two reasons: 1) learning the skill of writing a cogent argument is essential in the Common Core and, accordingly, in higher education and 2) argumentation calls upon three higher-order thinking skills: analysis, evaluation, and synthesis.

- **Analysis.** The words *analyze* and *analysis* appear in the Common Core State Standards document 292 times. The etymology of the word *analysis* illuminates its meaning: "to loosen up." To analyze something is to take it apart, to examine its parts and how they work together. Yes, an analysis is a breakdown, but it is more than just that. The skill of analysis also involves one step beyond breakdown, and that is an explanation of the relationship among the components. If you were to analyze a peanut-butter-and-jelly sandwich, for example, you'd be explaining how and why its three ingredients—peanut butter, jelly, bread—blend to produce the whole gustatory effect.
- **Evaluation.** Evaluation comes into play in writing argument in two underlying ways. First, the student needs to evaluate sources of information. The Common Core stresses the importance of this skill (Reading Standards 6, 8). Next, the student needs to make decisions about what evidence to include as well as how and where to include it to mount an argument that will be effective for the targeted audience.
- **Synthesis.** Synthesis, now at the top of the food chain of thinking skills, is the culminating skill of argumentation. The student has to select relevant, cogent facts and put them together in a logical order, using effective diction (ie., words with the desired connotation and tone). Coming back to our peanut-butter-and-jelly sandwich, an act of synthesis would

be going to the grocery store, knowing where to find the ingredients, and then using criteria to select just the right kind and brand of peanut butter, jelly, and bread for the intended lucky recipient.

Analysis does not require evaluation or synthesis. Evaluation requires analysis but not synthesis. Synthesis requires both analysis and evaluation, which is why mounting an argument is considered such an important and complex skill. (Bloom's taxonomy, developed in 1956, was updated in the 1990s by Benjamin Bloom's protégé Lorin Anderson to crown "creativity" (aka synthesis) at the top of the thinking-skills pyramid.)

A Recommendation

The best resource I've seen about teaching argumentation is the little, easy-to-use book *They Say/I Say: The Moves that Matter in Academic Writing* (Gerald Graff and Cathy Birkenstein, Norton). The authors explain how argumentation involves entering into an existing conversation about an issue, acknowledging the opposition, and returning serves and volleys. Most usefully, they provide an index of templates—sentence frames for various kinds of arguments and parts of arguments. These sentence templates form a set of training wheels that get students going as writers of argument. They also include graceful ways of integrating quotations, which is most welcome, as the Common Core stresses writing from sources (Writing Standards 8, 9).

CHAPTER 8

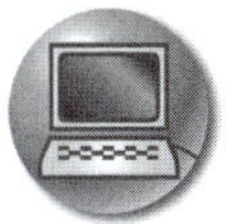

Formative and Summative Assessments

Usually when we hear the words *formative* and *summative*, we are talking about assessments. Formative assessments are diagnostic, giving the teacher information about how the class as a whole or students as individuals understand a particular concept or set of facts so far. For the teacher, formative assessment determines how things are working so far and what should be done next. Summative assessments are end-of-the-road tests that are used for formal purposes, such as ranking students against each other. While summative assessments affect a teacher's gradebook and a student's report card, formative assessments affect a teacher's planbook and a student's notebook.

We would like to switch things around a bit and get you thinking about formative and summative *skills*, rather than assessment. Formative skills are those that affect a student's notebook. These would be the *study skills* that help students learn along the way—things students can do to help them focus, organize information, remember facts and formulas, and construct learning as they read. The Common Core does not name a set of study skills, but students must develop study skills to reach the Common Core goals. Summative skills, on the other hand, are skills that result in evidence of learning that will be directly assessed, either by a teacher or by the anonymous evaluators of high-stakes tests.

To combine sports and music analogies, formative skills are applied in *practice, warm-ups* and *rehearsal*; summative skills are the *game* or *concert*. As applied to the Common Core, a formative skill would be the ability to outline a chapter from a textbook; a summative skill would be the ability to produce an oral or written summary of reading material. A formative skill would be the ability to compose appropriate questions for an interview with a school board member about what it is like to serve on a school board; a summative skill would be to conduct the actual interview and report on it, either in speech or in writing. And a formative skill would be to look up a word in a dictionary, find the appropriate definition for a given context, and also look up any words in the dictionary definition that impede comprehension; a summative skill would be the ability to actually use the word in a meaningful way.

Too often in education, we head students who have insufficient formative skills straight for the summative assessment. It is the formative skills that lead up to the summative skills, the ones being assessed. Let's break down the Common Core State Standards in terms of formative and summative skills.

Formative and Summative Skills of Writing

Except for the most informal of written communication (texting, Facebooking, tweeting, writing on a bathroom wall), writing is not just speech written down. College and career writing must adhere to the codes of formal (or at least semi-formal) Standard Written English (SWE). The best formative skill that leads to writing is reading. Just as you would not expect a musician to write an opera without having heard a variety of operas over and over again, you can't expect students to write in a genre in which they are inexperienced. So, the first step in meeting the Common Core's Writing Standards for argument, information, and narrative is to read argument, information, and narrative. The next step is to analyze argument, information, and narrative texts: *What are their parts? How are they organized? What distinguishes them from each other? How do you know which one of the three a given text is? What kinds of words do they use?* So, students not only have to read arguments, information, and narratives, they have to—with your help—build awareness of the key features of these three genres so they can replicate them in their own writing. And, yes, that is why it takes a full K–12 education to learn the skill of writing in these three genres!

Types and Purposes

1. **Write arguments.**

Formative skills. Read editorials and persuasive speeches.

- Learn the parts of an effective argument and be able to identify them in an editorial or persuasive speech.
- Understand how writers of editorials and persuasive speeches repeat their thesis statements by changing the wording in several strategic places throughout their arguments.

Summative skills. Write a well-developed, age-appropriate persuasive essay on a meaningful topic that requires outside information, not just opinion.

2. **Write informative/explanatory texts.**

   Formative skills. Read encyclopedia and magazine articles that have a purely explanatory purpose.

   Summative skills. Write a well-developed report. The two salient features of report writing are that it uses language sparingly and it is well-organized enough to be converted into (and from) an outline. When we say that reporters use language sparingly, we don't mean that the report itself has to be very short: we mean that the sentences themselves should be lean and mean—packing the most information into the fewest words. The organization of a report goes from general to specific. The reader of a report can stop reading at any point without losing the most important information, which is not the case with an argument or a story.

3. **Write narratives.**

   Formative skills. Read stories, both fiction and nonfiction. Learn how to use quotation marks to capture direct speech. Learn how to tell and write an anecdote.

   Summative skills. Write stories. These may be fictionalized or true accounts, or a combination.

Production and Distribution

4. **Match your style to the expectations of the audience.**

   Formative skills. Express information using informal (conversational) language. Identify the words and phrases that need to be more formal (business-like).

   Summative skills. Convert information from informal to formal language register.

5. **Use the writing process.**

   Formative skills. Engage in a prewriting activity, such as listing. Formulate a draft. Revise the content by adding and deleting. Edit by correcting surface errors.

   Summative skills. Complete a polished piece of writing that has been carefully developed over time, with evidence of the planning and changes that a polished piece of writing results from.

6. **Use technology as a collaborative tool.**

Formative skills. Students are already using technology as a collaborative tool for writing (perhaps too much!) as they text, Facebook, e-mail, instant message, and Twitter. They need to advance and deepen their tech-based communication to include more intellectual input. This can include going through the process of solving a math problem, studying for a fact-based test, or responding to an editorial.

Summative skills. Create and contribute to a class blog that requires extended, serious response (more than a Tweet) to topics that are more important than pop culture.

Following are rubrics for the three kinds of writing: narrative, informational, and argumentation. These rubrics follow the Grades 6–12 CCSS Writing Standards 1–6. The rubric for narrative writing would be used for English language arts writing only; the rubrics for writing information and argument would be used not only by English language arts teachers, but also by teachers of history, social studies, science, and technical subjects, as designated by the Common Core. You will notice that individual grade levels are not given. If you teach the lower end of the 6–12 grade span, you might want to make appropriate adjustments to the expectations for students at your level. (Reproducible versions of these rubrics are available in Appendix B on page 165.)

Figure 8.1. Writing Rubric: Common Core State Standards, Grades 6–12:
English Language Arts — Type: Narrative

	PRE-NOVICE	NOVICE	SEMI-PRO	PRO
Writing an introduction	Does not succeed in engaging the reader; is vague and/or disorienting	Makes some noticeable attempt to engage the reader by establishing a setting, characters, and/or situation	Makes contact with the reader by establishing at least two of the following: character, setting, situation	Effectively engages and orients the reader by establishing a context and introducing a narrator and/or characters: organizes an event sequence that unfolds naturally and logically
Using narrative technique	No or little use of narrative techniques such as dialogue, description, pacing, characterization, conflict	Limited but noticeable use of more than one narrative technique, such as dialogue, pacing, description, characterization, conflict	Good start toward use of more than one narrative technique, such as dialogue, pacing, description, characterization, conflict	Engaging use of such narrative techniques as dialogue, pacing, description, characterization, conflict

	PRE-NOVICE	NOVICE	SEMI-PRO	PRO
Sequencing and transitioning	All or mostly simple sentences with no or very few transition words and conjunctions used; No paragraphing	Uses only the most basic transitional devices (words, punctuation, phrases, clauses, paragraphs) to convey shifts in time and space	Uses some transitional devices (words, punctuation, phrases, clauses, paragraphs, section divisions) to convey shifts in time and space	Uses a variety of transitional devices (words, punctuation, phrases, clauses, paragraphs, section division) to convey shifts in time and space
Vocabulary	Word choice does not show effort at being interesting and precise.	Glimmers of use of words that are interesting, lively, precise, accurate, striking, dramatic to create characters, setting, and conflict	Good start at using words that are interesting, lively, precise, accurate, striking, dramatic to create characters, setting, and conflict	Strong use of words that are interesting, lively, precise, accurate, striking, dramatic to create characters, setting, and conflict
Using formal writing tone	Overall tone is too informal, including some or all of: "texting" abbreviations, slang, messiness, errors in spelling, punctuation, grammar; no attempt to use dialect to capture the speech of characters	Attempt at formal writing style, but needs more proofreading and/or care in presentation; attempt at using dialect to capture the speech of characters	Good attempt at blending formal English conventions (spelling, grammar, punctuation, capitalization) with dialect to capture the speech of the characters	Excellent blend of formal English conventions (spelling, grammar, punctuation, capitalization) with dialect to capture the speech of the characters
Writing a conclusion	No or very sketchy conclusion	Some attempt at a conclusion that leaves the reader with a sense of closure	Good start toward a strong conclusion that leaves the reader with a sense of closure	Strong conclusion that rewards the reader for having read the story

Developed by Amy Benjamin in accordance with the Common Core State Standards for Literacy in English Language Arts and Social Studies, Science, Technical Subjects, www.amybenjamin.com

Figure 8.2. Writing Rubric: Common Core State Standards, Grades 6–12:
English Language Arts and Literacy for History, Social Studies, Science, and Technical Subjects — Type: Informational

	PRE-NOVICE	NOVICE	SEMI-PRO	PRO
Writing an introduction	Effectively does NEITHER of the following: Clarify the topic; Preview how it will be developed	Effectively does ONE of the following: Clarify the topic; Preview how it will be developed	Effectively does BOTH of the following: Clarify the topic; Preview how it will be developed	Effectively does BOTH of the following: Clarify the topic; Preview how it will be developed with headings and sub-headings
Explaining the information	No or few relevant facts, definitions, concrete details, quotations, examples	Some relevant facts, definitions, concrete details, quotations, examples	Good start toward presenting relevant facts, definitions, concrete details, quotations, examples	Thorough presentation of facts, including graphics such as well-explained charts, tables, and/or other visuals
Expressing relationships between ideas	All or mostly simple sentences with no or very few transition words and conjunctions used; No paragraphing	A few organizational structures and transitional words	Transitions from paragraph to paragraph, but needs more internal transition and linkage within paragraphs	Establishes clear and effective organization through paragraphing, sectioning, complex sentences, transitions and other linking devices
Using Tier II and III vocabulary	No Tier II or III vocabulary used	Some Tier II and III vocabulary used	Tier II and III vocabulary is evident, but there are several instances where Tier II vocabulary should be used instead of Tier I	Sufficient, appropriate use of Tier II and III language throughout
Language tone	Overall tone is too informal, including some or all of: "texting" abbreviations, slang, messiness, errors in spelling, punctuation, grammar	Attempt at formal writing style, but needs more proofreading and/or care in presentation	Good attempt at formal writing style and proofreading, but a few glaring errors indicate that more careful proofreading is needed	Formal writing tone used throughout; Few or no glaring errors in spelling, grammar, punctuation, capitalization; obvious care in presentation
Writing a conclusion	No or very sketchy conclusion	Some attempt at a conclusion that leaves the reader with a sense of closure	Good start toward a strong conclusion that explains the importance of the information	Strong conclusion that clearly summarizes the information and explains its importance
Developed by Amy Benjamin in accordance with the Common Core State Standards for Literacy in English Language Arts and Social Studies, Science, Technical Subjects, www.amybenjamin.com				

Figure 8.3. Writing Rubric: Common Core State Standards, Grades 6–12:
English Language Arts and Literacy for History, Social Studies, Science, and Technical Subjects — Type: Argumentation

	PRE-NOVICE	NOVICE	SEMI-PRO	PRO
Writing an introduction	Effectively does NONE of the following: State importance of issue; Make a claim; Acknowledge opposing claim	Effectively does ONE of the following: State importance of issue; Make a claim; Acknowledge opposing claim(s)	Effectively does TWO of the following: State importance of issue; Make a claim; Acknowledge opposing claim(s)	Effectively does ALL of the following: State importance of issue; Make a claim; Acknowledge opposing claim(s)
Developing an argument	No relevant facts, statistics, reasons, or evidence	Mentions, but does not develop, sufficient evidence; Does not attend to opposing claim(s)	Good start toward developing claims and opposing claims; Includes some substantial evidence	Develops claims and opposing claims thoroughly and fairly with evidence: facts, stats, reasons, examples, anecdotes
Expressing relationships between ideas	All or mostly simple sentences with no or very few transition words and conjunctions used; No paragraphing	A few organizational structures and transitional words	Transitions from paragraph to paragraph, but needs more internal transition and linkage within paragraphs	Establishes clear and effective organization through paragraphing, sectioning, complex sentences, transitions and other linking devices
Using Tier II and III vocabulary	No Tier II or III vocabulary used	Some Tier II and III vocabulary used	Tier II and III vocabulary are evident, but there are several instances where Tier II vocabulary should be used instead of Tier I	Sufficient, appropriate use of Tier II and III language throughout
Using formal writing tone	Overall tone is too informal, including some or all of: "texting" abbreviations, slang, messiness, errors in spelling, punctuation, grammar	Attempt at formal writing style, but needs more proofreading and/or care in presentation	Good attempt at formal writing style and proofreading, but a few glaring errors indicate that more careful proofreading is needed	Formal writing tone used throughout; Few or no glaring errors in spelling, grammar, punctuation, capitalization; obvious care in presentation
Writing a conclusion	No conclusion	Sketchy conclusion that just restates the claim and/or the issue; does not make an impact on the reader	Good start toward a strong conclusion that follows from the evidence and makes an impact on the reader	Strong conclusion that follows from the evidence presented and makes an impact on the reader

Developed by Amy Benjamin in accordance with the Common Core State Standards for Literacy in English Language Arts and Social Studies, Science, Technical Subjects, www.amybenjamin.com

Conclusion: Writing

Writing is both an expression of what we know (a form of assessment) and a means of learning (a form of processing, or constructing knowledge). Not all student writing needs to be formal and edited. Not all student writing needs to culminate in having someone read what the student wrote, much less evaluate it.

For students to be ready for college, they need to develop the habit of marshaling their learning by taking notes from lecture and readings. They also need to already have proficient skills in formal standard English—colleges are not known for teaching those skills; colleges are known for expecting them. As for the world of work, while not everyone writes regularly on the job, almost everyone will need to present themselves respectably in writing if they aspire to the full range of options in any field.

The first Classroom Close-Up that follows illuminates how teachers can use the assignment itself to improve student writing. The second shows how a music teacher incorporates literacy as a means of learning music.

CLASSROOM CLOSE-UPS for Writing

Mapping and Framing Writing

I (Michael) was recently speaking with an English teacher about the Common Core and the process of writing. She recalled an encounter she had while tutoring after school.

> I was working with a student who was given an assignment to explain a quotation. The only directions given were to write a paragraph of at least six sentences explaining the meaning of the quotation. He had some things written down before we started. Most of the page was filled with what really could have (and should have) been stated in one to two sentences. However, we had a long way to go because he did not understand the quote—it was metaphorical and he was taking it literally.

She went on to voice her frustration with the teacher: how the instructions were so vague, how there was a lack of a structure and helpful modeling for the assignment. I include this brief encounter because her point is so valid. When discussing written work, teachers often complain about students' poor performance: specifically, how often students repeat themselves meaninglessly. But what these teachers fail to realize is that writing should be a learning experience for the student, not just an assessment or a demonstration of knowledge. It should be an exercise in formulating knowledge, getting to understand what they think in the process of expressing it.

To alleviate teacher frustration, assessments involving writing should be previewed by instruction on *how* to write. Students need a framework for writing academically. Such a framework can be achieved through many means, and the Common Core State Standards can help. Mr. Burke has established a comprehensive structure to create better student writers. His system, which he calls TORT, helps students learn the art and skill in writing that is applicable to all disciplines. Here is his story.

Over the last three years, I have been challenged, as an educator, to produce AP-quality work from my high school students. My district added an AP world history class and eliminated the honors classes, resulting in increased enrollment of students with ranging talents, according to the College Board standards.

Understanding that the College Board's AP World History Exam is extremely challenging (three essays and 70 multiple-choice questions), I entered the 2010 academic year with great expectations. Although the students had scored well the previous year, I wasn't satisfied with the overall results. Additionally, throughout that academic year, I found that my students could recall pertinent facts but left them out of their essay responses. Frustrated, I would continuously reiterate that they knew far more than their papers indicated. I began to reflect on my teaching, wondering if there was more that I could do to ensure greater success. I realized that my students needed a structured way to learn to write clearly, enabling them to document all the information they knew. So I developed TORT.

TORT is a structured guideline for writing. It enables students to create a comprehensive and well-written first paragraph of an essay. TORTing allows for students to maintain a content-driven point of argument while keeping the required focus of the assessment. By using this strategy, students can first learn how to address the question and then demonstrate what they know about the subject. TORT has truly revolutionized the way I teach writing to my students. It has taken on a life of its own.

Below is a breakdown of the TORT process. It is important to reiterate that TORT is a writing strategy to develop the first paragraph of an essay. This "TORTed" opening provides a guided structure for the remainder of the essay, enabling the student to write with greater depth and breadth.

The TORT Formula

T: Topic sentence

The opening sentence of the essay should be definitive, specifically including a definition of the most important word from the task/question. Students are asked to include a time period and region in this sentence or the next. (Note: Specifying time and region always applies to social studies writing, but does not necessarily apply to other subject areas. For example: If the thematic essay on the New York State Regents Examination in Global Studies and Geography revolves around the topic of nationalism, a student using TORT would open the essay by defining the word *nationalism*. Next, they would set the stage for the essay by naming the region and time period relevant to the nationalistic movements they are about to discuss.

O: Opinion or argument

The argument or opinion component of TORT is what is conventionally referred to as the thesis statement. It is the driving statement from which the essay is created and establishes the argument the student is trying to prove, which is why it is considered *opinion*. Students must be specifically instructed not to use *I, me,* or *my* here. (Although writing in the first person is perfectly legitimate in other genres, social studies teachers are notorious for disliking it. Students, on the other hand, are notorious for using it. Writing in the first person comes naturally, which is why students default to it. If we want to be successful in steering students away from use of first person in an academic essay, we need to offer specific examples of how to express opinion in the third person.)

For example: Using the above essay on nationalism, the student would state that leaders (e.g., Ghandhi of India or Napoleon Bonaparte of France) used the strong feeling of nationalism to lead historic movements in their respective nations, inspiring and influencing people in nations around the world.

R: Reason Number 1

The following sentence consists of justification of the Opinion (O); it is a valid reason (R) that backs the student's support for the thesis.

For example: The student would cite in a sentence or two specific actions by which the particular leaders supported the spread of Indian nationalism or French nationalism, respectively.

R: Reason Number 2

The student's next sentence cites further specific examples and additional support for the student's opinion/argument.

T: Transitional/closing sentence

Students can give a short answer to the original prompt/task/question and/or create a transitional sentence to move their essay into the first body paragraph.

So the first paragraph of the essay is now complete using the TORT method. To recap, an opening sentence was created that pinpoints what is most important from the assigned task (Topic). Next, an opinion or argument is established by the student (Opinion). The following two or three sentences are plugged in, citing specific examples to support the opinion (Reasons). Finally, a transitional sentence closes the paragraph and moves to the body paragraphs (Transition).

This formula works for almost any topic. Whether it be content-driven academic information or a persuasive position paper, by following the above format, students can establish a talking point and the position they wish to take and provide support for their opinion—all in the first paragraph. This solid opening sets the stage for the remainder of the essay and gives the writer credibility.

Once the students have mastered this introduction, it will be necessary to introduce the process of fleshing out the reasons (Rs) in the body paragraphs of the essay. Each reason (R) from the TORT introduction will become the foundation for each body paragraph. Depending on the complexity of the question or task, it might be necessary for students to state three or four reasons (Rs) to support their opinion (O). Thus, the TORT could become TORRRT or TORRRRT. Consequently, the more reasons (Rs) given to support the opinion (O), the more body paragraphs needed to answer the task (three paragraphs for TORRRT and four paragraphs for TORRRRT).

In each body paragraph, students should provide two or three examples that support each reason (R). They should clearly state their reason and use good transitional words to connect the reason to the example. After sufficiently describing and using examples to back their reasons within the body paragraphs, students need a concluding paragraph. In the conclusion, they should restate their claims and provide one last illustration of deeper analytical thought.

TORTing needs to be introduced in stages and should be developed over time so that answers can become more analytical. Students will be required to write often. Once TORTing is taught, all work moving forward should follow it. Although TORTing was originally developed to address the needs of AP students, Mr. Burke has used it for all academic levels. He relayed the following account:

> Recently, I gave a written assessment in class, allowing only one 41-minute period to complete it. A student exclaimed, "I'm lucky I can write a paragraph in 41 minutes, let alone a complete essay!" As the bell sounded to finish the exam period, she handed me a beautifully written essay. She said, "I used TORT, and everything came together like a puzzle. I was surprised how much I remembered!" That is the point exactly! These students have so much content stored, they just can't express it. Now, with TORT, they have a structured way to write to their highest level.

The application of a structure like TORT provides students with a formulaic approach to writing, aka *scaffolding*. With such a roadmap, the process of writing becomes more manageable and less exhausting. Students simply plug content into TORT and create a paragraph that paves the way for the rest of the assignment. Because TORT is so flexible and applicable to any discipline, the writing process takes its place in students' procedural memory. They follow the routine for writing a comprehensive piece and focus on what information to include as opposed to how to make the pieces fit coherently (Sylwester, 2005, as cited in Armstrong, 2008, p. 100).

The TORT writing strategy lends itself beautifully to all aspects of the Common Core State Standards. TORT allows students to gather information from multiple sources and support, inform, and enrich their claim or position (Writing Standards 1, 2, 8 & 9). Teachers who use it can more easily create opportunities for students to write routinely because the TORT structure decreases student anxiety about the writing process and increases their efficiency when writing (Writing Standards 5 & 10). An important note: Because TORT is the strategy used to create only the first paragraph, it might not always be necessary for students to write the remainder of the essay. If students can take a position on a subject and provide a number of reasons to support their argument, all within one paragraph, the remainder of the essay would only provide further justification to their position. Therefore, in less than 10 minutes, teachers can provide students with the opportunity to write critically within their lessons. TORTing can be a routinely used instructional chunk to inculcate literacy skills because the information generated within a single paragraph is so inclusive.

Making Use of Literacy—Music to My Ears!

Mrs. Dena Tishim is just beginning her career teaching music and performance arts. In the lesson below, Mrs. Tishim makes use of literacy to explore the challenges of choral arrangement and performance. Similar to Mrs. Dellaposta's photography lesson (see p. 156), Mrs. Tishim tasks students to critically think about the development of a finished product—in this case, their sound and musical arrangement as a choral group. While reading through the lesson, note Mrs. Tishim's use of literacy to facilitate the practice of communication skills and problem solving.

Essential Question. How do we solve the musical challenges we encounter in our choral concert music?

Objectives. The students will be able to 1) identify difficult sections of our concert music and use content specific vocabulary to describe the problem, 2) use prior knowledge to come up with a solution for the problem, and 3) collaborate within each voice section to write a paragraph describing both the problem and the proposed solution.

Key Vocabulary. Stacatto, measure, solfege, chords, half-steps, rhythm, pitch, scale

Do Now. As the students prepare for their choral concert, the class will address topics of concert order, meaningful repertoire choice, historical significance, authentic performances based in research of style and period, and self-assessment of performance challenges.

I lead the students in group discussions of particular performance challenges within vocal parts and prescribe solutions for these challenges. After the students determine the difficult sections of the music, I use the students' prescribed solutions to fix each problem. If necessary, we explore other solutions. We discuss the success or failure of the students' solutions in the hope that they can continue to work toward solving musical performance problems.

Summarizer/Closure/Homework. The students will be able to read and comprehend a scholarly article from the New York Times. The students will use their reading-comprehension skills to summarize and analyze a review of a concert. Prior knowledge of attending and participating in concerts will serve as a reference point for students. Because the artists addressed in the article are part of pop culture, knowledge of them will help students to connect course content with real-world applications. I will read exemplary answers to encourage analytical thinking and clarity in expressing ideas related to content. Students will be expected to use prior knowledge and content-specific vocabulary to answer questions and respond to articles.

During Mrs. Tishim's choral lesson, she provides students the opportunity to practice literacy skills to increase the quality of her chorus' sound. Although the true betterment of vocal harmony and blending is attained as they rehearse and physically sing, it is important for students to critically think about these processes, to verbalize and visualize the finish product. However, students need time to develop these skills.

On the following page are a number of writing samples from one student in the bass section of the chorus. This young man describes the difficult parts of the musical selection "Over the Rainbow," and, as the lesson plan indicates, he attempts to provide some insight into possible solutions to those problem areas. Please note that the student's responses are in chronological order over a period of a few weeks. The student's insights are limited at first, but once comfortable with the processes of writing and analyzing the choral sound, the student begins to elaborate on his findings and offers specific explanations for resolution.

Piece: "Over the Rainbow"

Basses Example 1: Measures 79–80; working apart from the rest of the choir

Basses Example 2: The pitch for beats 1 & 2 in measure 23 is difficult to attain. If reminded that the pitch is lower, we may reach it.

Basses Example 3: The most difficult sections of "Over the Rainbow" are the *Oo's*. The musical challenge is that we might not always start on the correct pitch and the staggered breathing. To solve this problem we can work on it during the lessons or during class. We could work on the starting pitch and on how long to keep the right pitch.

Basses Example 4: The musical challenge of the *fa la la* is the counting so that we know where we are. Also the fast-paced melody is a challenge for some of the basses. During the lessons, we could work on the song at a slower pace and as we acclimate to the song, we could pick up the pace. Then we could add the sopranos and altos and see how it sounds. If it does not work, then we could just slow down the pace until we get it right. Then, eventually, we will be at a normal pace.

What a beautiful progression the student makes in his use of literacy and his ability to clearly state difficulties and possible solutions! Before reading this close up, one might think, "How can I realistically implement literacy practice into a choral lesson?" I include this lesson as a classroom close-up for three reasons. First, it is a unique and creative way of practicing literacy. Second, because it contains elements of literacy found within the CCSS Standards for Writing (Standards 1–5, 8 & 10). Finally, as evidenced by the student's earlier writings (little elaboration, no posed solutions), it is important to recognize that the successful implementation of literacy within a unit or lesson plan does not take place overnight; inculcating literacy skill in students takes time.

Mrs. Tishim's lesson and the writing assignment she assigns for homework provide practice for literacy. By routinely implementing time to write, especially in a music course, students gain confidence in their skill and ability to communicate clearly and effectively.

Part 3

Speaking and Listening

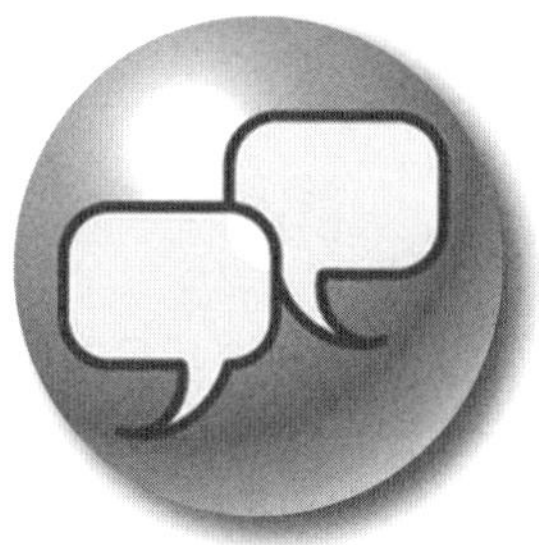

CHAPTER 9

Speaking and Listening and the Common Core

The third set of standards addresses speaking and listening in a variety of contexts, for a range of purposes, with different kinds of audiences.

Breaking Down the Standards

Below are simplified statements of the standards, followed by the original language (www.corestandards.org).

Comprehension and Collaboration

1. **Develop socially acceptable conversation skills. Prepare for and participate** effectively in a range of conversations and collaborations with diverse partners, building on others' ideas and expressing their own clearly and persuasively.
2. **Verbally summarize information that you've heard or read.** Integrate and evaluate information presented in diverse media and formats, including visually, quantitatively, and orally.
3. **Assess the credibility of what you read and hear.** Evaluate a speaker's point of view, reasoning, and use of evidence and rhetoric.

Presentation of Knowledge and Ideas

4. **Present meaningful ideas and information coherently and courteously.** Present information, findings, and supporting evidence such that listeners can follow the line of reasoning and the organization, development, and style are appropriate to task, purpose, and audience.

5. **Enhance formal presentations with visuals, including digital media.** Make strategic use of digital media and visual displays of data to express information and enhance understanding of presentations.

6. **Know the rules of formal spoken English and apply them when appropriate to the audience.** Adapt speech to a variety of contexts and communicative tasks, demonstrating command of formal English when indicated or appropriate.

Regarding the range and content of the Speaking and Listening Standards, the Common Core State Standards document (www.corestandards.org) says this:

> To become college and career ready, students must have ample opportunities to take part in a variety of rich, structured conversations—as part of a whole class, in small groups, and with a partner—built around important content in various domains. They must be able to contribute appropriately to these conversations, to make comparisons and contrasts, and to analyze and synthesize a multitude of ideas in accordance with the standards of evidence appropriate to a particular discipline. Whatever their intended major or profession, high school graduates will depend heavily on their ability to listen attentively to others so that they are able to build on others' meritorious ideas while expressing their own clearly and persuasively.
>
> New technologies have broadened and expanded the role that speaking and listening play in acquiring and sharing knowledge and have tightened their link to other forms of communication. The Internet has accelerated the speed at which connections between speaking, listening, reading, and writing can be made, requiring that students be ready to use these modalities nearly simultaneously. Technology itself is changing quickly, creating a new urgency for students to be adaptable in response to change. (Core Standards, p. 48)

Technologies such as texting, tweeting, blogging, e-mailing, and other forms of Internet-based person-to-person messaging crossbreed the conventions of writing and speech. The conventions of formal written English—punctuation, proper spelling, complete sentences—are certainly not expected and would, if applied, actually brand the user as an outsider, someone unfamiliar with the expectations of these forms. This development is neither good nor bad: We simply have evolved toward a form of writing that is more like speech that happens to be written down. Many people view this as a degeneration of the language, but it is, in fact, just another natural outgrowth of technology that makes sense for its purpose and audience.

There's no underestimating the importance of social communication in the twenty-first-century workplace and marketplace. As we become more globally networked with each passing day, the need for social communication skills becomes ever more ascendant as a workplace skill. The most promising jobs for today's students are those requiring social skills. It is social skills, combined with analytical smarts, that launches growth and innovation.

> Highly developed social skills are different from mere sociability. They include persuasion, social perceptiveness, the capacity to bring the right people together on a project, the ability to help develop other people, and a keen sense of empathy. These are quintessential leadership skills needed to innovate, mobilize resources, build effective organizations, and launch new firms. They are highly complementary to analytic skills—and indeed, the very highest-paying jobs (and the most robust economies) usually require exceptional skill in both realms. Nonetheless, social skills seem to grow ever more essential as local economies grow larger and more complex. In this sense, (social networks) are like brains: their growth and development require the growth and development of an increasingly dense web of synaptic connections. (Florida, 78)

This section is about ways to improve the quality and quantity of student and teacher talk in the classroom by holding instructional conversations rather than scripted Q&As. After dissecting the traditional model of classroom discourse, we will explore models that get more students involved in instructional conversations. In the next chapters, we'll look at these models:

- Whiteboarding
- Socratic seminar
- Fishbowl discussions
- Role playing

CHAPTER 10

Traditional Classroom Discourse: The Recitation Script

Teachers stand in front of the room and talk. They disseminate information, give directions, and ask questions, eliciting orderly responses from students who raise their hands for permission to deliver correct answers. (Or, in the case of my (Amy's) classroom, for permission to use the lavatory, consult with a guidance counselor, receive ministrations from the nurse, pick up the lunch that has been dropped off by Mom or Dad in the main office, request that the temperature in the room be adjusted, or ask me if tomorrow is going to be a snow day.) Since the days when Socrates wandered in the groves of academe trailed by his entourage of eager students, those who were not texting or Googling were participating in classroom discourse. In Soc's outdoor classroom, the discourse reputedly consisted of questions having open-ended answers that resulted in more questions. Language—classroom discourse—is the primary medium for teaching and learning.

Because oral language is the primary means of communication in the classroom, we educators should develop a more conscious understanding of its workings so that we can use it more intentionally. Courtney B. Cazden (*Classroom Discourse: The Language of Teaching and Learning*) describes three features of classroom discourse that affect learning:

1. **Language transmits curriculum.** It is primarily through language that we disseminate information and determine what students know and don't know. Students learn in the classroom primarily through listening; they

express what they know primarily through writing, and to some extent, through speech.

2. **Language communicates control.** A classroom is a group situation in which the teacher is expected to regulate what gets said, who says it to whom, and how loudly. When more than one person is speaking at the same time, when there are multiple conversations buzzing, some people get nervous. Yet, it is the irrepressible tendency of humans to talk, especially when they are acquainted and exciting things are happening around them. Cazden calls this tendency "simultaneous autonomous conversations" (p. 2) and it sure does take a great deal of energy to "keep a lid on it," as teachers are famously exhorted to do.

3. **Public language is a risk to personal identity.** We've all had the sensation of feeling our faces heat up when suddenly called upon to recite knowledge. Even the most outgoing person knows the excruciating discomfort of the risk of language. But students are not the only ones who can experience anxiety about speaking in public, teachers get anxious as well. The way to control that anxiety is to remain in control: to limit classroom discourse to safe and predictable responses, to minimize surprises. Yet doing that is what results in a deadened classroom atmosphere, one that does little to awaken or advance students.

Given the importance of language in the transmission of knowledge, the urgency of language among peers, and the vulnerability of a person expected to speak, how can we use oral language more effectively in the service of learning? How effective is what we usually do? Cazden notes that "the three-part sequence of teacher initiation, student response, teacher evaluation (IRE, also called the "recitation script"), is the most common pattern of classroom discourse at all grade levels, and that the teacher usually initiates the interaction using the question form" (p. 29). (Think of the classroom scene in *Ferris Beuller's Day Off* where Ben Stein, playing the teacher, drones, "Anyone ....? Anyone ...?") The recitation script model conveys the message that the teacher is in control, there are right and wrong answers, the students are being compliant when they deliver them, and their answers will be decisively and publicly judged. It's a Ping-Pong Q&A game where "designated hitters" keep the ball going. Those who are sure of themselves are in the game; those who are not are benchwarmers. As with "teaching" vocabulary and spelling by assigning lists of unrelated words to memorize, the IRE paradigm is not effective, but it remains in place because it is safe, orderly, and deeply traditional.

What are the shortcomings and alternatives to the recitation script? It makes students extremely passive, for one thing. They are answerers of questions that have answers, not seekers. Room for the insights and needs of students is not in this model. The recitation script does very little as a formative assessment, as it really does not communicate to the teacher what *most* of the students know or don't know. It's not interesting to most of the class, which is why most of the class is disengaged, one way or another. It lets nonparticipating students off the hook. It easily degenerates into a "Guess What I'm Thinking" game, as the teacher rejects unexpected responses. The recitation script is robotic, noninvestigatory, disengaging, predictable, shallow, and slow. Rather than inviting and furthering thought, it neatly and cleanly cuts knowledge into bite-sized pieces. Therefore, the recitation script is, by necessity, limited to lower cognitive processes, even though it is misleadingly labeled "class discussion."

A true class discussion would not involve just three or four students responding to low-level questions that have right or wrong answers. A true class discussion—a rarity, according to research—would involve a high level of engagement of most of the students, would involve disagreements, unanswerable questions, tentative answers, restatements of the assertions of others, attempts to clarify, and, most of all, spontaneity. A true classroom discussion would be difficult to keep on track, hard to control. But as a conversation rather than a recitation, it does meet the Common Core in every way.

Working With the Recitation Script Model

The disadvantages of the recitation script model are obvious, but we cannot possibly dismiss it altogether. We can improve it, and we can vary it.

- **Wait time.** Key to improving the quality of student responses is waiting for a response. The research by Cazden, as cited in Brophy and Good, reveals that "teachers typically wait one second or less for students to start a reply to their question before calling on another student or supplying information related to the question themselves, in what we'll call the 'Classroom as Quiz Show' model. Interestingly, in studies where teachers were asked to incorporate longer than typical wait times, that action led to 'more active participation in lessons by a larger percentage of the students.' [S]ubsequent research has verified that increasing wait time leads to longer and higher-quality student responses and participation by a greater number of students" (Brophy and Good, p. 377).
- **Think-Pair-Share.** In think-pair-share, students are given a moment to think about a question. Then they discuss it with a partner, and then they share further with either another pair or the whole class. Think-pair-share is a staple of cooperative learning developed by Professor Frank Lyman at the University of Maryland (1981).

- **Affective tone.** Students need to feel safe and valued if they can be expected to speak. When there's enmity between students for reasons outside the teacher's control, that is not going to happen, and there's not much you can do about it as a whole class. But you *can* have students work in self-selected groups.

There are times when the recitation script format seems like the only way to get to the point where everyone knows a set of facts they need to know before moving on to higher-level thinking. In my workshops with educators on the Common Core, for example, I need to be assured that everyone knows certain basic facts, and these facts may be less than fascinating as they are rolled out. I try to inject a little humor into an otherwise dry presentation by interspersing a little quiz show at intervals. Rather than doling out the facts and figures, I turn them into engaging questions that invite participation.

Sea of Talk

The Common Core document presents the six speaking and listening standards *after* the reading and writing standards, so that is the order we are following in this book. However, speaking and listening, as language capacities, are the prerequisites and foundations for the written word. That is why, in 1971, James Britton famously stated that "Reading and writing float on a sea of talk." It is the richness of the aural language (listening) that will shape the other three language capacities: speech, reading, and writing, in that order.

What kinds of listening and speaking experiences do students have in our classrooms? Whether a class is teacher dominated or student centered, students need to be exposed to, and given opportunities to use, the language of academics and business. Teacher-centered classrooms rely heavily on students listening to information dispensed by the teacher and reading (to some extent, though usually not enough). But if the teacher's language is not rich in Tier II and Tier III words* blended in a comprehensible way, the student's language will not become acclimated to the language expected of educated people. It is essential that teachers model the use of the Latin- and Greek-based words (Tier II and III, respectively), especially for students for whom school is the only place where they will hear such words. (*Note that Tier II words are generic academic words not ordinarily in basic conversational English but used across all subject areas and in business communications. Tier III words are technical words specific to a subject area. See Appendix C on page 169 for sample academic words.)

In a student-centered class, one where students are constructing knowledge by solving problems and working cooperatively, teachers still need to be a language resource through their own modeling. No one expands his or her language use without the opportunity to speak in a nonthreatening environment, but the opportunity to speak is not sufficient: Language is learned primarily though input, not output. According to language-acquisition expert Stephen Krashen (2004), language, whether a second language or new levels of one's native language, is acquired through comprehension of real messages when the acquirer is at ease (not on the defensive, not afraid of being judged). It is the teacher's job, then, whether in a teacher-centered or student-centered philosophy, to walk both sides of the street, providing enough familiar language to transition the listener to new language. It is comprehensible input of real messages that puts into motion the brain's unconscious acquisition of language.

> It does not occur overnight, however. Real language acquisition develops slowly, and speaking skills emerge significantly later than listening skills, even when conditions are perfect. The best methods are therefore those that supply 'comprehensible input' in low-anxiety situations, containing messages that students really want to hear. These methods do not force early production in the second (or first) language, but allow students to produce when they are 'ready,' recognizing that improvement comes from supplying communicative and comprehensible input, and not from forcing and correcting production. (Krashen, pp. 6–7)

Listening and speaking are behaviors of courtesy and respect without which we do not communicate productively. The standards themselves (See Speaking and Listening Standard 1) acknowledge the importance of social competencies, skills that facilitate interpersonal exchanges with a minimum amount of static and a maximum amount of fruitful understanding.

Next we'll discuss the elements and advantages of Socratic dialogue in the classroom, with its emphasis on open-ended questions, finding evidence and referring to it, and active listening. We describe a cooperative learning technique called whiteboarding. Socratic dialoguing and whiteboarding move us beyond scripted recitation, promoting a more independent, if less predictable, way of learning.

CHAPTER 11

Moving Toward Socratic Dialogue

As everyone knows, Socrates taught by asking questions and more questions, leading his students to discover their own answers, answers that would only be subjected to more questions. Today we call this method Socratic dialogue or Socratic seminar, a highly valued method of engaging students in real learning.

Following is a glimpse at three kinds of classroom discourse at three levels of effectiveness (Wenning, 2005, p. 3).

Scripted Recitation

Teacher: Who can tell me the equation that we would use to figure out the acceleration, given initial velocity, final velocity, and distance?

Student: You'd find the difference between the final velocity squared and the initial velocity squared. Divide that by two times the distance.

Teacher: Good. That's right. It's v-final squared minus v-initial squared divided by 2x.

We've already pointed out the disadvantages of the scripted recitation model. The following example, called "funneling" (Wood, 1998, as cited in Wenning), involves some probing of thinking processes. In funneling, the teacher uses wait time and scaffolding questions to shape students' thinking.

Funneling

Teacher: I've dropped a ball that was in a resting state from a given height. What would be the speed of the ball when it is 5 meters below the point from which I've dropped it?

(Long pause—no response from the students)

Teacher: OK, let's see how we can approach this problem. What do we know about the acceleration of the ball?

Students: It's 9.8 meters per second squared.

Teacher: That's right. Would we be looking for an average speed or an instantaneous speed?

Students: Instantaneous. We need to know the speed of the ball when it is 5 meters— exactly—below the point of release.

Teacher: That's right. Then how can we determine the speed at this exact point?

(Long pause—no response from the students)

Teacher: Well, talk this over with your partner: What equation do we use that relates instantaneous speed and distance?

Students: Is it the v-squared equation?

Teacher: Yes, the v-final squared minus v-initial squared divided by 2gx, where g is the acceleration and x is the distance.

Students: So, solve for x; we know that acceleration equals 9.8 meters per second squared, right?

Teacher: That's it, yes!

In the dialogue, the funneling process begins when the students respond to the teacher's second question. To get the students to arrive at a predetermined conclusion (the desired equation), the teacher asks a series of questions that point the way through the logical steps. But the person doing the thinking is the teacher, with the students producing answers to what (to them) are simple questions. This is not problem solving; it is answer giving. There's a difference between answer giving and problem solving.

Students who learn well by following a model may learn to problem solve through funneling. But as long as the thinking that supports the teacher's series of easier questions is known only to the teacher, most students will not learn to problem-solve through the funneling method of questioning. It is not enough for students to answer the funneled questions: They need to understand the reason why the teacher frames the problem by asking these particular questions.

The third model, focusing (Wood, 1998, as cited in Wenning), comes closest to true Socratic dialogue. In this kind of classroom discourse, the teacher listens analytically to students' answers and asks follow-up questions that promote clarification for the students of their own thinking as they express what they know (or think they know). The goal of focusing the questions in this way is to get the students to learn the process of problem-solving by reflecting on their own thinking.

Focusing

Teacher: I've dropped a ball that was in a resting state from a given height. What is the speed of the ball when it is 5 meters below the drop point?

(Long pause—no response from the students)

Teacher: How would a physicist go about solving a problem like this? What would be the first questions?

Students: We would have to relate the given variables to the unknown.

Teacher: Yes, and what are the given variables? What is or are the unknown(s)?

Students: The ball started at rest. That's a given.

Teacher: And? What is the relevance of the fact that the ball started at rest?

Students: That means its initial velocity was zero.

Teacher: What is the initial acceleration?

Students: It's not going anywhere to start, so zero.

Teacher: Well, how would you define acceleration?

Students: Acceleration is the speed. The velocity.

Teacher: Do acceleration and velocity mean the same thing?

Students: No, acceleration is the rate of speed. Acceleration is the rate of velocity.

Teacher (acting like he's mulling this over): Hmmm … the rate of velocity.

Students: Acceleration is the rate of change of velocity.

Teacher (still acting mystified): OK, so if acceleration is the rate of change of velocity, which it is, and if the ball has no velocity to start, how can its velocity undergo a change in its rate?

Students: Oh, right. The ball has to have a nonzero acceleration, or it won't move at all.

Teacher: Now you're onto something. So what else do we know?

Students: We know the distance is 5 meters.

Teacher: The distance of what?

Students: The distance that the ball has supposedly fallen that we're looking for the final velocity for.

Teacher: If the ball is going to keep on falling, which it will, how is the distance at 5 meters the final velocity? Let's say the distance from the top of the—let's say it's a bridge—to the water is 15 meters.

Students: We're looking for the speed at 5 meters exactly.

Teacher: What is the word we use to describe speed at an exact point?

Students: Instantaneous velocity.

Teacher: Yes. OK, so we have acceleration, initial velocity, and distance of fall. We want to find the instantaneous velocity. Do we have everything we need?

Students: Yes, we should be good to solve.

Teacher: So what now? How are the variables related?

Students: So v-final squared minus v-initial squared divided by 2gx, where g is the acceleration and x is the distance.

Teacher: Explain why you chose that equation. Why didn't you use the equation that says distance equals one-half g t-squared?

Students: We can't use that equation because t-squared is an unknown. Our equation has to have only one unknown.

Teacher: Good thinking. So we throw all the known quantities into the first equation. We solve for the single unknown. What do we get? Assume that gravity causes an acceleration that is 10 meters per second squared.

Students: 10 meters per second, downward.

Teacher: That's it! We did it!

Wenning (2005) explains the importance of valuing both problem and process.

> When the students provide answers to questions, the teacher asks for conceptual clarifications of statements or explanations of intellectual processes. The focus here is on the process of solving the problem as well as actually solving the problem itself. Process and product are equally valued. Only if the teacher focuses students' attention on the process of problem solving will they come to understand how to reason their way through such a process. Thinking is made explicit. This also helps the teacher to identify, confront, and resolve any misconceptions that students might have, and helps students learn problem solving through vicarious experiences. (p. 8)

Implementing a Socratic Seminar

The instructional framework known as *Socratic seminar* works a bit differently from the Socratic dialogue we described above. This type of question-driven dialogue works well for fact-based subjects like physics and math, where students need to understand how formulas work and how they are connected to problems. The purpose of Socratic seminar is to generate thought and improve comprehension through close reading of a short text that the group has read together. The students read a short text in class, with or without introductory commentary by the teacher. The teacher asks questions that can be answered only by finding evidence in the text. The evidence may be directly stated or implied, and the questions may have more than one answer, *but the students have to point to specific words in the text to support their answers.*

A popular and well-respected sequential program fostering Socratic seminar for middle and high school students is called "Starting Off Strong" by The Great Books Foundation. What follows is an encapsulation of how a teacher might wade gradually but surely into the waters of a full-fledged Socratic seminar. Using a series of four texts accompanied by seminars of increasing depth, each a full class period long, teacher and students can acclimate themselves to a format of learning that differs significantly from traditional classroom discourse.

First Seminar. In this first classroom experience with Socratic seminar, you explain that a seminar differs from a traditional class in that a seminar is about the students talking, not the teacher talking. Explain that everyone will be reading a short text and then exploring their own ideas about it by looking again at the text to respond to your questions. Your questions can be answered in various ways and by several people. You are not looking for a single right answer. Rather, you are looking to see what they find in the text in response to your questions.

The seminar has to be set up with students in a circle, facing each other. You have to be sitting, not standing. These physical cues are important to establish the seminar's student-centered nature and to cue the difference between the traditional role of the teacher giving information and the Socratic role. You will ask them to read the text once, take a few notes or make annotations, share their notes and thoughts with a partner, and then read the text again. Now it's time for your questions that scaffold the seminar. Avoid "So what did you think about it?" questions (see box on page 97). Your first round of questions should be ones that focus students on meaning. Here are some possible opening questions:

- What do you think the author wanted you to come away with after reading this? How do you know?
- What might be controversial (upsetting, unsettling, disturbing, offensive, infuriating) about this text?
- Where in the text might someone have a negative reaction or disagree?

Note that we are not asking the students to explain their own differing points of view at this point. To do so might be worthwhile, but not for this type of seminar. Here, we want students to focus on the meaning—explicit and implied—of the text itself. Avoid the temptation to turn the seminar into an issue-driven debate, as that will surely become polarizing—dominated by one or two students, off-putting to others, and, most importantly, distracting from the text itself.

As you ask these questions, keep in mind that they are genuine questions, questions for which you do not anticipate a particular answer. Be open to unanticipated answers. Respond neutrally; that is, check yourself against responses that convey "liking" or "not liking" a student's response. Thank the student for responding, and ask for justification: "Why do you say that?" "How do you know?" And, most importantly: "Show us in the text." Give everyone a chance to find the place in the text that the student is using as justification. Because you will be asking students to locate specific lines in the text to justify their responses, it's a good idea to number every five lines in the margins.

TIP: Establish a Purpose for the Seminar

It's important to reinforce that the purpose of the seminar is not to express a liking or disliking of the text itself. Comments like "It was boring" or "It was stupid" are conversation enders that do nothing to advance understanding of the text. Emphasize that statements about whether you "liked" the text are irrelevant to whether you understand it and know whether or how others understand it. Because "I liked it" or "I didn't like it" are the default responses to texts, works of art, and experiences, it takes some paradigm shifting to move students away from such responses and into analytical responses.

This is what a Socratic seminar on the prologue to *Romeo and Juliet* might look like with an experienced teacher and class.

Two households, both alike in dignity,
  In fair Verona, where we lay our scene,
From ancient grudge break to new mutiny,
  Where civil blood makes civil hands unclean.
From forth the fatal loins of these two foes
  A pair of star-cross'd lovers take their life;
Whose misadventured piteous overthrows
  Do with their death bury their parents' strife.
The fearful passage of their death-mark'd love,
  And the continuance of their parents' rage,
Which, but their children's end, nought could remove,
  Is now the two hours' traffic of our stage;
The which if you with patient ears attend,
  What here shall miss, our toil shall strive to mend.

Teacher: What contrasts do you notice?

Possible responses: two different households; children and parents; old fighting and new fighting; two enemies; love and rage

The prologue gives us information about what the play is going to be about: a fight between two families, young lovers who take their own lives, the resolution of the feud because of that, the fact that the young lovers are acting out their destiny ("star-cross'd"). What information is not given to us?

The Socratic seminar works best if the text is short—a few pages at most, perhaps as short as a paragraph or sonnet-length poem. If the text is much longer than a few pages, it will be unwieldy to have the students flipping through pages and pages to find justification for their answers.

Socratic seminar does not take the place of direct instruction or even a limited amount of scripted recitation. It is, rather, an alternate way of interacting with the text. Unlike traditional instruction, Socratic seminar does not seek to arrive at closure. It seeks to raise questions that stimulate thinking. The questions must refer the reader back into the text, but that does not mean that the questions have definitive answers. What we are looking for is evidence that can support assertions. The teacher's responses should be nonjudgmental, probing for evidence that justifies an assertion. Responses like "Why do you say that?" "How do you know?" "Say more about that." "Show us in the text where you justify that," are appropriate for Socratic seminar rather than responses like "Very good!" "Yes that's right!" or "Good thinking!" It's hard to transition from judgmental or overtly encouraging responses to neutral ones that just probe for deeper reflection.

Think of the Socratic seminar format as a set of teaching skills that you can blend into your study of texts. Socratic seminar is not an all-or-nothing thing. Depending on the text, your objectives, and how the students react with each other, you can select the elements of Socratic seminar that work well for a given topic and class.

CHAPTER 12

Developing Social Competencies

The first of the Common Core State Standards for Speaking and Listening establishes the need to teach students at all grade levels to "prepare and participate effectively in a range of conversations and collaborations with diverse partners, building on others' ideas and expressing their own clearly and persuasively." Explaining further, the authors of the standards stipulate what everyone knows intuitively about proper functioning in the workplace, and, arguably, in college:

> To become college and career ready, students must have ample opportunities to take part in a variety of rich, structured conversations—as part of a whole class, in small groups, and with a partner—built around important content in various domains. They must be able to contribute appropriately to these conversations ... Whatever their intended major or profession, high school graduates will depend heavily on their ability to listen attentively to others so that they are able to build on others' meritorious ideas while expressing their own clearly and persuasively. (p. 48)

In other words, we are expected to teach students to behave in a courteous manner. Courtesy is the bedrock of *effective* speaking and listening. In an atmosphere of discourtesy, humans revert to a primitive state of self-preservation: a fight-or-flight response that marshals human energy away from the direction of intellectual advancement, to say the least. Discourtesy results in the kind of stress that launches the individual either into aggressiveness or withdrawal unless he or she is socially skillful enough to breach the negativity. Learning thrives in an atmosphere of mutual respect, which engenders a sense of safety. A sense of safety frees the conscious mind to evaluate opposing ideas, accept new information objectively, and formulate coherent thoughts both mentally and verbally.

It goes without saying that everyone connected with education wants students to behave courteously in the classroom and throughout the school. Most educators understand the reciprocal nature of courtesy, and they model respectful interactions with students, which are, for the most part, returned in kind. But the problem, as I see it, is that in many classrooms and schools, courteous behavior in the learning environment is viewed as something to be desired, maybe even expected, but not enforced.

It may seem oxymoronic to use the phrase "enforced courtesy," but that is exactly what happens in the workplace. Try any of these things at a meeting being led by your boss and note the response: Put your head down on the desk and close your eyes. Lean back on your chair, focusing all your concentration on balancing yourself on one chair leg. Text incessantly. Enter into a giggling fit with your buddies, and kick it up a notch when glared at. At a key point in a discussion, ask to be recognized and then say something relevant only to your personal needs. Disappear for long intervals. Belch. Keep your coat on. Wear a frayed ball cap. Stretch your legs out and set up your personal belongings in the aisles. Stroll in late and then disrupt proceedings by demanding to be brought up to speed. Complain and demand. Ask, "Do we have to know this?" Roll your eyes. Yawn ostentatiously. Arrange your face in a blank stare, a look of mild annoyance, or an outright sneer. Keep your arms folded. Never have a writing implement. Show disdain for peers. Snap gum, blow bubbles until they pop on your nose, then ask for a tissue. Let guests know that they are imposing on your routine. Eat whatever you want, wherever you want, as loudly as you want. Place no restraints on your desire to engage in social conversations with those in your immediate vicinity as well as those across the room. Do whatever you can to create a diversion or derail the focus of the meeting. And, by all means, use obscenities without provocation. A few minutes before the meeting is scheduled to end, pack up noisily, remind the boss that time's up, and gather with your friends in the doorway.

Although everyone deplores, or is at least mildly annoyed, by the above discourtesies, they certainly flourish—hopefully not all at once—in classrooms, hallways, and auditoriums. And yet, destructive as crass behavior will eventually be to those who never learn otherwise, we often abdicate our responsibility to insist on appropriate conduct, as though it is not our business or our job to do so. "Pick your battles" is the usual advice when it comes to calling out shabby manners, as though "small" offenses like the ones just mentioned are not worth confronting. But the "broken window" hypothesis of social behavior in public places holds that if we attend to seemingly small matters, we can maintain a level of civility that inevitably deteriorates once we start ignoring quality-of-life issues—the so-called small stuff. Malcolm Gladwell explores this notion that "disorder invites more disorder."

> In a famous experiment conducted ... by the Stanford University psychologist Philip Zimbardo, a car was parked on a street in Palo Alto, where it sat untouched for a week. At the same time, Zimbardo had an identical car parked in a roughly comparable neighborhood in the Bronx, only in this case the license plates were removed and the hood was propped open. Within a day, it was stripped. Then, in a final twist, Zimbardo smashed one of the Palo Alto car's windows with a sledgehammer. Within a few hours, that car, too, was destroyed. Zimbardo's point was ... that a small deviation from the norm can set into motion a cascade of vandalism and criminality. The broken window was the tipping point.
>
> The broken-window hypothesis was the inspiration for the cleanup of the subway system conducted by the New York City Transit Authority in the late eighties and early nineties. Why was the Transit Authority so intent on removing graffiti from every car and cracking down on the people who leaped over turnstiles without paying? Because those two "trivial" problems were thought to be tipping points—broken windows—that invited far more serious crimes. (from Gladwell's "The Tipping Point" essay in *The New Yorker* on June 3, 1996)

Now, surely, there has to be hope for improving the level of civility and respect for people and property in your classroom and school if New York City, aboveground and below, was able to undergo the transformation that it has.

The fact is, not to travel too far afield from the point, *social skills affect learning.* Consider the applicability to the Common Core State Standards in Speaking and Listening of these assertions by The National Association of School Psychologists (NASP).

> Good social skills are critical to successful functioning in life. These skills enable us to know what to say, how to make good choices, and how to behave in diverse situations. The extent to which children and adolescents possess good social skills can

> influence their academic performance … While most children pick up positive skills through their everyday interactions with adults and peers, it is important that educators … reinforce this casual learning with direct and indirect instruction. We must also recognize when and where children pick up behaviors that might be detrimental to their development or safety. In the past, schools have relied exclusively on families to teach children important interpersonal and conflict-resolution skills. However, increased negative societal influences and demands on family life make it imperative that schools partner with parents to facilitate this social learning process. This is particularly true today given the critical role that social skills play in maintaining a positive school environment. … With a full repertoire of social skills, students will have the ability to make social choices that will strengthen their interpersonal relationships and facilitate success in school. (NASP Fact Sheet, 1999)

There's a relationship between poor social skills and poor academic performance. According to the NASP, "Students with poor social skills have been shown to

- Experience difficulties in interpersonal relationships with parents, teachers, and peers.
- Evoke highly negative responses from others that lead to high levels of peer rejection.
- Show signs of depression, aggression, and anxiety.
- Demonstrate poor academic performance as an indirect consequence.
- Show a higher incidence of involvement in the criminal justice system as adults."

The classroom is an organic (living, breathing, in-the-moment) community in which everyone's energy creates a positive or negative learning environment. We can all agree, but what can we do about it? Social skills need to be addressed, but not by individual teachers swimming upstream alone. These skills need to be named and promoted by the school (district, community) as a whole. What follows are several research-based published interventions with good track records for improving social skills in school.

- **"Stop and Think" Social Skills Program** (Knoff, 2001, p. 3). Part of Project ACHIEVE (Knoff and Batche). Has demonstrated success in reducing student discipline referrals to the principal's office, school suspensions, and expulsions; fostering positive school climates and prosocial interactions; increasing students' on-task behavior; and improving academic performance. (www.projectachieve.info)

- **Primary Mental Health Project** (Cowen et al., 1996, as cited in NASP). Targets children K–3 and addresses social and emotional problems that interfere with effective learning. It has been shown to improve learning and social skills, reduce shyness and anxious behaviors, and increase frustration tolerances. http://www.sharingsuccess.ort/code/eptw/profiles/48.html
- **The EQUIP Program** (Gibbs, Potter, & Goldstein, 1995). Offers a three-part intervention method for working with antisocial or behavior-disordered adolescents. The approach includes training in moral judgment, anger management/correction of thinking errors, and prosocial skills. (www.reserachpress.com/scripts/product.asp?item=4848#5134)
- **The PREPARE Curriculum** (Goldstein, 1999). Presents a series of 10 course-length interventions grouped into three areas: reducing aggression, reducing stress, and reducing prejudice. It is designed for use with middle school and high school students but can be adapted for use with younger students. (www.researchpress.com/scripts/product/asp?itme=5063)
- **The Accepts Program** (Walker et al., as cited in NASP). Offers a complete curriculum for teaching effective social skills to students at middle and high school levels. The program teaches peer-to-peer skills, student-to-adult skills, and self-management skills. (www.proedinc.com/customer/productView.aspxs?) (www.naspoline.org/resources/factsheets/socialskills fs.aspx)

Source: NASP Fact Sheet

The collective behavior of students (or any group of people) establishes norms. We can have all the rules we want in our Code of Conduct booklet, but it is the actual behavior (the norms) that determine culture and climate. Whether a student's (or students') poor social skills stem from lack of knowledge, lack of impulse control, lack of practice, lack of consequences for negative behavior, or plain old cantankerousness, we will never create productive speaking and listening environments in our classrooms without addressing social skills. Social skill development is not optional or tangential to the Common Core State Standards. The first standard for speaking and listening calls for students to learn how to communicate *effectively* in a variety of circumstances.

CHAPTER 13

Whiteboarding

Student-sized whiteboards are simply miniatures of the large whiteboards that you use with dry erase markers in your classroom. What we are calling "whiteboarding" is a classroom practice in which students, working together or individually, show their work on the whiteboard and then use it as a visual in their explanation to small groups or the whole class. It's a simple, inexpensive, convenient device that actually has tremendous instructional value in getting students to engage in just the kind of activities that meet the Common Core State Standards for Speaking and Listening.

Professor Carl J. Wenning (2005) of the Physics Teacher Education Program at Illinois State University in Normal, Illinois, has written extensively on the uses of whiteboarding to have students work through their understanding of physics problems and explain their thinking processes and procedures. "It (whiteboarding) is an instrument well suited to improving the quality and quantity of scientific discourse in a classroom" (p. 3). Professor Wenning teaches the use of whiteboarding in this way:

> Typically a cooperative inquiry-oriented project is assigned to student groups. Students explain their findings and ideally will provide multiple representations of the understanding they have developed. The floor is then opened to questions. Teachers and students are allowed to seek clarifications and justifications for student conclusions. Using the whiteboarding approach, teachers hope to change students from "collectors of

> information to expectatant creators of … coherent understanding" (Wells, Hestenes, & Swackhamer, 1995 in Wenning, p. 3). Whiteboarding is strongly associated with the pedagogical approach known as Socratic dialoguing. (Wenning, p. 3)

Whiteboarding not only addresses the speaking and listening standards of literacy for the Common Core, it is also in keeping with standards for communication in math and science, as set forth by the National Council of Teachers of Mathematics (2000) and the National Science Education Standards (1996). These bodies recognize the importance of being able to communicate scientific/mathematical ideas coherently among peers. Communication skills in math and science do more than transmit ideas from one person to another: the act of using language is in itself a meaning-making activity.

Of course, whiteboarding is a slightly new way to do a very old thing, as Wenning reminds us.

> In many ways, whiteboarding is a tried-and-true method that fell by the wayside with the advent of more sophisticated classroom technology. In many ways, whiteboarding harkens back to the days of the one-room schoolhouse where every student had his or her own slate board and chalk for writing, drawing, and computation, and was responsible for sharing with the teacher and fellow students the work that he or she had done. The teaching approaches used with whiteboards today are much more effective. (p. 3)

Wenning specifies ways in which whiteboarding "is an effective approach for teachers implementing three research-based principles identified by the National Research Council (2000, 2005) as critical to learning.

1. **Engaging students' prior understandings.** This is critical to the development of scientific thought and central to the teaching approaches known as constructivism and concept change. Whiteboarding provides a canvas for a student's line of reasoning, allowing any flawed reasoning or inaccurate information to be identified.

Constructivism

Constructivism is defined as the process of creating one's own learning through mental activity or the educational theory that posits that learning takes place through bridging new to known information. The concept-change theory of education posits that learning occurs when cognitive dissonance requires us to stop and adjust our notions (preconceptions) to accommodate new information.

2. **Relating factual knowledge and conceptual frameworks in understanding.** Through whiteboarding, teachers provide a medium for inquiry-oriented lessons while facilitating classroom discourse, evaluation, and interpretation of evidence. Students get to know *how* they know *what* they know. When we consider the small proportion of knowledge that it is possible to learn within the walls of the classroom and within the time constraints of formal schooling, we have to acknowledge that learning how to learn is among the most valuable skills students can acquire.
3. **Emphasizing the importance of student self-assessment and autoregulation.** Again, we're talking about students taking charge of their own learning beyond the school day and school years. Few things are more motivating than the knowledge that you have to face your peers and account for your work. Yet, the anxiety of doing so is lessened when one is working as a member of a team.

Whiteboarding is a way to make a classroom learner-centered, subject-centered, (formative) assessment-centered, and language-centered. Whiteboarding is a much richer learning experience than student reporting.

> Whiteboarding (and student reporting) actually have different purposes. The report is a presentation intended to demonstrate competence and is usually graded. Whiteboarding, on the other hand, is an active learning (and collaborative) process in which evaluation is a (formative) process designed to probe a student's prior understanding and to construct strategies to bring the student to a more complete comprehension. (Yost, 2003, in Wenning, p. 5)

Whereas reports are one-way expressions, whiteboard presentations include substantial interaction between teachers, the students presenting, and members of the class. Unlike mere reporting, whiteboarding requires that students provide evidence-based justification for their conclusions.

In their book *Classroom Strategies that Work*, Robert J. Marzano, Debra Pickering, and Jane E. Pollack (2004) recommend nonverbal processing as an effective strategy for fostering durable learning. Whiteboarding is the perfect vehicle for nonverbal processing when students use it to create graphic representations of concepts such as flow charts, equations and formulas, labeled diagrams, and models.

Another benefit of whiteboarding is its ability to use color as a learning tool. As most people are visual learners, color supports learning by imprinting an image in the memory. Through color, we facilitate understanding of, as well as communication about, complex systems and how their components interact.

The usefulness of whiteboarding as a learning tool is not limited to science and math. In social studies, students can use whiteboarding to create maps, timelines, flow charts, and graphs. In English language arts, whiteboarding can be used to show sentence diagrams, storyboards, character webs, and semantic maps.

Whiteboarding is an inexpensive, convenient, accessible way to engage students in the verbal-communication skills required for college and career readiness. (For more on whiteboarding, see page 158).

Conclusion: Speaking and Listening

Speaking and listening are social competencies. The kind of speaking and listening required by the Common Core is not haphazard. We need to think professionally about how speaking and listening are developed in our schools and plan learning experiences that allow students to function intelligently in a group. Just as we scaffold reading and writing, we need to do so with academic speaking and listening. According to Cynthia McCallister (2011), developer of Learning Cultures (www.learningcultures.org):

> It is a uniquely human capacity to work collaboratively in relatively extensive social groups to accomplish common goals. … Our special brain power enables us to understand the mental states of others, and thereby manage differences, exploit collective strengths, solve problems creatively, and achieve our imaginative possibilities. Our capacity to use language essentially to think how others think allows remarkable individual and group achievements. We're wired to overcome obstacles by reaching out to others in order to solve problems and pursue our goals. (p. 110)

CLASSROOM CLOSE-UPS for Speaking and Listening

Socrates' Ideas of Listening and Speaking

"He who questions much, does and discusses much, shall learn much."—Sir Francis Bacon

Christine Miller is a conscientious veteran teacher who is currently pursuing her National Board Teaching Certification. She is a master at lesson and unit preparation, making use of a variety of instructional strategies that call upon literacy skill. A consistent focus of her daily instruction centers around improving reading, writing and speaking skills. Below is an instructional exercise, her take on the Socratic seminar, that she uses to build students' communication acumen.

The Socratic seminar, named after the Greek philosopher Socrates, utilizes an inquiry-based approach to learning. It is a very useful instructional strategy when studying a topic with various interpretations or perspectives. Very student centered, the seminar promotes critical thinking and encourages divergent thoughts. It enables students to apply many of the essential academic and literacy skills: listening, speaking, discussing, inquiring, and thinking critically.

In preparation for conducting a Socratic seminar, students read a given document such as a segment from a textbook or a primary- or secondary-source selection. Students analyze the document and organize it into appropriate categories (this categorization piece is a flexible component of the exercise—depending on the nature of the reading and the discipline studied, this should be modified to meet the needs of the student and the material). It is beneficial to allow students to prepare for the seminar in small groups using a jigsaw or a round-robin exercise, which promotes small-group discussion and builds student confidence when sharing the analysis of ideas. After reading the text, students are asked to create approximately four critical-thinking questions (both close and open-ended questions, questions that make global connections and societal comparisons).

I use a rubric to assess student preparation and performance during the seminar. Expectations are clearly delineated and exemplars are provided so students under-

> stand their role(s) during the seminar. Specific behaviors are listed in the rubric, such as speaking loudly and clearly, citing reasons and evidence for their statements, listening to others respectfully, sticking with the subject and/or asking appropriate questions, paraphrasing accurately, communicating effectively with one another (not just the teacher), and general preparation practices.
>
> There are many different ways to arrange a Socratic seminar. A useful technique, referred to as "the fishbowl," works well and encourages active participation from all students. In the fishbowl, students are partnered before the seminar begins. Each "team" caucuses, focusing on two to four specific behaviors listed in the rubric. For the first few seminars, it is appropriate for the teacher to provide the specific behaviors that peers should assess during the seminar. However, as students become comfortable with the process, they create a list of behaviors on which to focus (these areas are gleaned from teacher grades and comments from previous seminars). Peer analysis of behaviors also provides students with the opportunity for reflective practice, which promotes growth as well.
>
> For the seminar, the classroom is arranged into two circles, with one member of each two-person team sitting on the inside of the circle (the fishbowl), and the other sitting on the outer circle. Students in the fishbowl actively participate and speak during the seminar. Those on the outside assess their partner's performance and take notes on topics like a critical point in the discussion that needs to be made or expanded upon or a question that should be posed. At any given time, the teacher can ask for students to switch with their partners. Because the fishbowl creates a small, intimate discussion group on the inside, students are willing to participate. Meanwhile, on the outside, students must remain actively engaged in completing their tasks of partner assessment and documentation of discussion points. A "hot seat" (an empty chair) can be created in the middle of the inside circle for students who want to pose a compelling point. After voicing their perspective, students return to their seats.

To begin the dialogue, the teacher asks an open-ended question and then steps back to allow the discussion to evolve among the students. At first, the teacher must lead the discussion, but eventually, the students facilitate their own discussion. Naturally, the instructor must effectively prepare questions to fuel the seminar and work diligently to steer the conversation should it be necessary.

Kids are curious and social by nature. Using any strategy centered on the inquiry approach, such as the Socratic seminar, fuels an interactive constructive learning experience. In addition, it provides students with many opportunities to practice and hone literacy and communication skills—a mainstay of the objectives found throughout the literacy standards for the Common Core.

Providing students with the opportunity to read text, speak at length on a topic, pose arguments, and counter their classmates' points affords them authentic and engaging practice with literacy. In preparation for the seminar, students must negotiate and comprehend complex text, reading closely for themes and main ideas, analyzing how details contribute to the material's overall meaning—skills found in the Anchor Standards for Reading (1, 2, 4 & 5). Additionally, they must maintain a position, and, most specifically, summarize and assess perspective and present their argument in a meaningful and coherent manner—skills seen in the Anchor Standard for Speaking and Listening (2–4 & 6). Finally, students are tasked to accurately judge their audience, make use of content-specific vocabulary, and expand their grasp of the English language as listeners (Language Standards 1, 3, 6).

Students enrolled in Mrs. Miller's classes effectively practice the skills stressed in the Common Core. Central to her philosophy on instruction is the focus on the development of students' essential literacy skill set. Every activity, specifically the Socratic seminar, provides an opportunity to hone skills that are universally important to student academic success—skills that are applicable to all disciplines and necessary outside of the confines of school. To approach instruction with a focus on skill and the use of curricula to inculcate literacy—this is the push of the Common Core and should be the goal of every practitioner in every school building throughout the nation.

The Four Corners

I (Michael) recently observed Ms. Alison Laino's Grade 9 global studies history and geography course. Teaching for only four years, Ms. Laino is dedicated to bettering her instruction and motivating her students with interactive and fun lessons. One strategy she uses, the four-corners method, has become a mainstay in her instructional toolbox.

On the day of my visit, Ms. Laino's instruction centered on the AIM (goal of the lesson): "How do the achievements of the Romans and the Greeks compare?" Throughout the lesson, she and her students worked diligently through a lecturette, a group work component and whole-group instruction using a graphic organizer. As this productive lesson reached its final 12 minutes, Ms. Laino posted the following statement on the electronic whiteboard: "The Romans' achievements are greater than the Greeks' achievements." She asked her students to write the statement in their notebooks and provide a detailed explanation justifying their position while taking one of four stances: *I strongly agree, I agree, I disagree, I strongly disagree.* She later spoke to me regarding this portion of the exercise.

> While the students are writing, I circulate and survey where they stand on the statement. I usually tell them that the more justification they give to back up their ideas, the easier it will be for them to discern their exact position. After they are finished writing, I take a poll and ask them to raise their hands as I announce each position. For many students, the polling heightens their level of participation because their choices are corroborated by their classmates, making them more comfortable with the position they chose.

Ms. Laino labeled each corner of her classroom (*I strongly agree, I agree, I disagree, I strongly disagree*). She asked for volunteers to occupy each corner and prepare to defend their position. Those students who did not volunteer were instructed to remain quiet until the end of the presentations. However, they were asked to add details to their position as they listened. Students in each corner of the room voiced their opinions, and a small debate ensued. Ms. Laino later added

> I often take the role of devil's advocate as the debate heats up. My questions and retorts probe students to delve deeper into analysis and critical thought to further back up their position. My little pokes and prods add fuel to the fire of an often lively discussion or, sometimes, an argument! I also like to use this activity as an activator to connect prior knowledge or as an assessment tool for the lesson's summarizer.

The students spoke eloquently, stating their positions, making points and counterpoints based on the arguments of other students. As the debate came to an end, Ms. Laino briefly reviewed the information that was covered in the lesson and commended the students' efforts.

When discussing the merits of the four-corners exercise and its connection with the Common Core State Standards, it is important to note that, much like Mr. Burke's three-minute drill, the four-corners strategy is only a component of a full lesson.

In this lesson, Ms. Laino accomplishes many instructional goals before employing the four-corners strategy. She successfully establishes foundational knowledge and has the students work through a variety of exercises to negotiate the content. While reading, keep in mind one of the sacred rules of instruction: make use of a variety of instructional strategies and chunk each lesson with multiple mini-lessons. Doing so results in a fruitful classroom.

The statement Ms. Laino writes on the board creates an avenue for students to evaluate and make judgments regarding the intricacies of the content. Anderson (2001), cognitive psychologist and former student of Benjamin Bloom, argues that such assessments, those that force students to evaluate and justify their positions, employ the highest forms of critical thought. Most relevant here,

Ms. Laino accomplishes this by assessing her students' justifications through three different modalities, all of which are staples of literacy in the Common Core State Standards. First, let us discuss the Anchor Standards for Writing.

Initially, Ms. Laino provides the means for students to write their position, (Writing Standards 1 & 5). She asks that students add to their arguments as they hear others present, fostering their ability to gather information from multiple sources and judge the accuracy of those sources (Standard 8). Because this is a rather routine instructional strategy used in her classroom, Ms. Laino can use the writing component as a tool to assess students' knowledge of the content, as well as their ability to apply that knowledge in the written word (Standard 10).

Because the students are presenting to an audience of their peers, there is a natural connection to the Anchor Standards of Speaking and Listening and Language as well. Elements of the comprehension and collaboration components of the Common Core are highlighted, particularly when asking students to assess the credibility of what they read or hear (Speaking and Listening Standard 3). Presenting meaningful ideas and information coherently and appropriately applying the rules of formal English to an audience are also some of the skills encapsulated in the four-corners exercise (Speaking and Listening Standards 4 & 6, Language Standards 1, 3, 6).

Part 4

Language

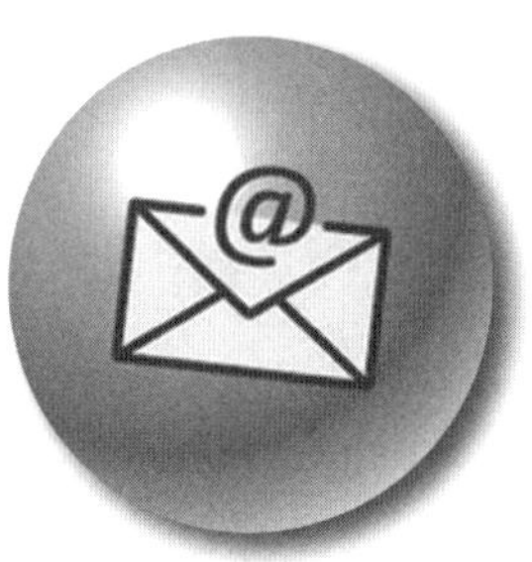

CHAPTER 14

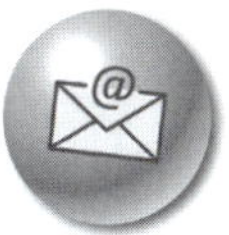

Language and the Common Core

The six language standards center on cultivating an academic and business-like tone over the years of a student's K–12 education. The language standards, especially the first three (which pertain to grammar) comprise the content of what English language arts teachers are expected to teach. As you can see, these standards actually outline a much-needed scope and sequence for grammar instruction at grade levels 6–12. Standards 4 and 5 address vocabulary in a way that applies primarily to English language arts teachers. Standard 6 addresses vocabulary and language use (choices in how we express ourselves) that apply directly to all subjects. Really, all of the six language standards are folded into the standards that precede them.

Breaking Down the Standards

Below are simplified statements of the standards, followed by the original language (www.corestandards.org).

Conventions of Standard English

1. **Know the rules of standard written and spoken English and use them when your audience expects you to do so.** Demonstrate command of the conventions of standard English grammar and usage when writing or speaking.

(Grade 6)

a. Ensure that pronouns are in the proper case (subjective, objective, possessive).
b. Use intensive pronouns (e.g., *myself, ourselves*).
c. Recognize and correct inappropriate shifts in pronoun number and person.
d. Recognize and correct vague pronouns (ie., ones with unclear or ambiguous antecedents).

(Grade 7)

e. Explain the function of phrases and clauses in general and their function in specific sentences.
f. Choose among simple, compound, complex, and compound-complex sentences to signal differing relationships among ideas.
g. Place phrases and clauses within a sentence, recognizing and correcting misplaced and dangling modifiers.

(Grade 8)

h. Explain the function of verbals (gerunds, participles, infinitives) in general and their function in particular sentences.
i. Form and use verbs in the indicative, imperative, interrogative, conditional, and subjunctive moods.
j. Recognize and correct inappropriate shifts in verb voice and mood.

(Grades 9–10)

k. Use parallel structure.
l. Use various types of phrases (noun, verb, adjectival, adverbial, participial, prepositional, absolute) to convey specific meanings and add variety and interest to writing or presentations.

(Grades 11–12)

m. Apply the understanding that usage is a matter of convention, can change over time, and is sometimes contested.
n. Resolve issues of complex or contested usage, consulting references (e.g. Merriam Webster's *Dictionary of English Usage, Garner's Modern American Usage*) as needed.

2. **The following includes the visuals of writing: capitalization, punctuation, and spelling.**

(Grade 6)

a. Use punctuation (commas, parentheses, dashes) to set off nonrestrictive/parenthetical elements.
b. Spell correctly. (Note that this applies to all grade levels, so we will not be repeating it: just be aware that spelling is not a forgotten Standard as we travel up the grade levels.)

(Grade 7)

c. Use a comma to separate coordinate adjectives.

(Grade 8)

d. Use punctuation (comma, ellipsis, dash) to indicate a pause or break.
e. Use an ellipsis to indicate an omission.

(Grades 9–10)

f. Use a semicolon (and perhaps a conjunctive adverb) to link two or more closely related independent clauses.
g. Use a colon to introduce a list or quotation.

(Grades 11–12)

h. Observe the hyphenation conventions.

3. **Knowledge of Language:** Understand that language is a changeable social contract, subject to legitimate disagreement about diction and usage depending upon audience, purpose, and level of formality.

(Grade 6)

a. Vary sentence structure patterns for meaning, reader/listener interest, and style.
b. Maintain consistency in style and tone.

(Grade 7)

c. Choose language that expresses ideas precisely and concisely, recognizing and eliminating wordiness and redundancy.

(Grade 8)

d. Use verbs in the active and passive voice and in the conditional and subjunctive mood to achieve particular effects (e.g., emphasizing the actor or the action; expressing uncertainty or describing a state contrary to fact).

(Grades 9–10)

e. Write and edit work so that it conforms to the guidelines in a style manual (e.g., *MLA Handbook*, Turabian's *Manual for Writers*) appropriate for the discipline and writing type.

(Grades 11–12)

f. Vary syntax for effect, consulting references (e.g., Tufte's *Artful Sentences*) for guidance as needed; apply an understanding of syntax to the study of complex texts when reading.

4. **Vocabulary Acquisition and Use: Use context, word parts, dictionaries, and other reference tools to figure out the meaning of words and phrases.** Determine or clarify the meaning of unknown and multiple-meaning words and phrases based on grade-level reading and content.

(Grades 6–12)

a. Use context (e.g., the overall meaning of a sentence or paragraph; a word's position or function in a sentence) as a clue to the meaning of a word or phrase.
b. Use common, grade-appropriate Greek or Latin affixes and roots as clues to the meaning of a word (e.g., audience, auditory, audible; belligerent, bellicose, rebel; precede, recede, secede; analyze, analysis, analytical; advocate, advocacy; conceive, conception, conceivable).
c. Consult general and specialized reference materials (e.g., dictionaries, glossaries, thesauruses), both print and digital, to find the pronunciation of a word or determine or clarify its precise meaning, its part of speech, or its etymology.
d. Verify the preliminary determination of the meaning of a word or phrase (e.g., by checking the inferred meaning in context or in a dictionary).

5. **Understand that words can have multiple meanings, connotations, and other subtleties.** Demonstrate an understanding of figurative language, word relationships, and nuances in word meanings.

(Grades 6–12)

a. Interpret figures of speech (e.g., personification, allusions, verbal irony, puns, euphemisms, oxymoron, hyperbole, paradox) in context and analyze their role in the text.
b. Use the relationship between particular words (e.g., cause/effect, part/whole, item/category, synonym/antonym, analogy) to better understand each of the words.

c. Distinguish among the connotations (associations) of words with similar denotations (definitions) (e.g., stingy, scrimping, economical, unwasteful, thrifty, frugal, prudent, conservative).

6. **Understand and use an academic/businesslike level of vocabulary and grammar.** Acquire and use accurately general academic and domain-specific words and phrases, sufficient for reading, writing, speaking, and listening at the college- and career-readiness level; demonstrate independence in gathering vocabulary knowledge when considering a word or phrase important to comprehension or expression.

CHAPTER 15

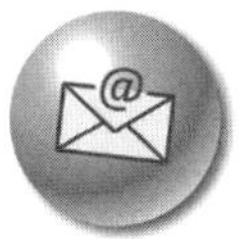

Grammar and the Common Core

Grammar instruction—whether done formally by English language arts teachers or incidentally by teachers of other subjects—has been problematic for many decades. Why? What's the problem? Two issues have to do with educational philosophy. Another is that teachers, including and especially English teachers, lack the knowledge and preparedness necessary to teach grammar effectively. Many English teachers feel unprepared to teach grammar because the state of grammar instruction when they went to school was not any better than what it is now. A teacher or two here and there took a stab at formal grammar, but a coherent scope and sequence was not in place. In some cases, a scope and sequence was in place, but it was taught in isolation rather than being integrated right into the "sexier" language arts, reading and writing. So grammar, even if it was taught, was shunted to the side, leaving a legion of English teachers today who sheepishly admit to either not knowing it well enough to teach it or not knowing any effective teaching models for grammar.

We're identifying two problems as "educational philosophy." 1) The traditional way of teaching grammar by having students do fill-in-the-blank worksheets identifying parts of speech/functions in a sentence, and correct-the-errors is just not a good way to learn. Ask anyone. The students do the worksheets and exercises, but they do not apply what they've learned to their writing or speech. They also do not remember what they "learned" from year to year, necessitating a "start all over again" curriculum that usually is shot through with holes created in the absence of instruction by grammar-averse teachers. 2) It has long been believed that grammar instruction needs to be applied directly to student writing, but in the absence of a coherent curriculum that is taught through sound pedagogy (not worksheets and exercises), students and teachers continue to work in the dark. What students do know about grammar is often too rigid and narrow to be useful, and it doesn't describe the English language the way it actually is.

The amount of grammar instruction consigned to English language arts teachers is clearly delineated in the standards, and, having worked with English teachers by the thousands, I feel confident in declaring that more than a few of them will find that list daunting. Lacking an alternative, they will no doubt reach for the nearest workbook. Students may or may not do well on weekly tests on grammar, but, if history is any indicator, there will be negligible transfer to the real world of language.

What everyone wants to know is how to integrate grammar instruction into the writing process, so that grammar is not taught as an add-on. Figure 15.1 illustrates how to actually apply knowledge of the parts of speech to writing in progress. English teachers should use this information by focusing on a particular part of speech when students have already written a rough draft and as they are about to revise.

Figure 15.1. How Knowing about Parts of Speech Fits into the Writing Process

If the writer knows about...	...then the writer is empowered to consciously and purposefully do the following:
Nouns	**Content and Style**
Beyond "person, place or thing": ▪ If you can put "the" in front of a word and have it make sense, then that word is a noun. ▪ If you can pluralize a word, then that word is a noun. ▪ If you can insert a word (phrase or clause) into the subject, object, or object-of-a-preposition slot of a sentence, then that word is a noun. ▪ If a word (phrase or clause) answers the question *Who?* or *What?* then that word (phrase or clause) is a noun (noun phrase or noun clause). ▪ If you can replace a word (phrase or clause) with the word *something* or *someone*, then that word (phrase or clause) is a noun (noun phrase or noun clause). ▪ A noun phrase is a noun plus the modifiers that come before and/or after it. ▪ A noun clause is a clause (subject plus verb unit) that does the work of a noun	Create a proper mix of generalities and specifics by using the right combination of common, proper, and abstract nouns. Create readable text by following the principle of short subject-long predicate. Add detail by expanding noun phrases, adding modifiers (adjectives, prepositional phrases, adjective phrases, adjective clauses) both before and after the head noun Create imagery. Use appositives to clarify and expand a noun; use appositives to be more concise (sentence combining). Adhere to the principle that sentences will come alive if the subject is a person who is animated by an action verb rather than a subject that is an abstract idea. **Surface corrections:** Capitalize proper nouns. Achieve subject-verb agreement. Achieve pronoun-antecedent agreement.

If the writer knows about...	...then the writer is empowered to consciously and purposefully do the following:
Verbs	**Content and Style**
Beyond "word that expresses action or state of being": Change the tense of the sentence. Whatever word changed is the verb. If there is a helping verb, this method will identify it, thus pointing up the beginning of the verb phrase. Any verb can have *-ing* added to it. Not all verbs are on duty as verbs. Off-duty verbs can act as adjectives (*a climbing vine*), or nouns (*Climbing is fun; I like to climb trees*.) A verb form (either *-ing* or the form of the verb that we use with the helping verb *have*) doing adjective work is called a *participle*. A verb form acting as a noun is called a *gerund*. A verb with *to* right in front of it is an *infinitive*. Participles, gerunds, and infinitives are called *verbals*.	Make effective and conscious decisions about when to use action verbs and when to use linking verbs. Eliminate clutter by selecting the right verb. **Surface corrections:** Use the proper verb tense; keep the verb tense consistent. Achieve subject-verb agreement. Use verbals to create parallel structure.
Adjectives	**Content and Style**
Beyond "modifies a noun": If a word answers one of the following questions, then it is an adjective (adjective phrase or adjective clause): ▪ What kind? ▪ Which one? ▪ How many? If a word can fit into the following frame, then that word is an adjective: The _______thing.	Eliminate unnecessary adjectives. Choose a noun that does not need the adjective. Create adjectival phrases and clauses that add detail and sentence variety. **Surface corrections:** Use a comma between adjectives that can be reversed; do not use commas between adjectives that cannot be reversed. (Variation: If you can put *and* between two adjectives, then you do need the comma.) Understand that possessive nouns function as adjectives, not as plural nouns (hence the apostrophe).

If the writer knows about...	...then the writer is empowered to consciously and purposefully do the following:
Adverbs	**Content and Style**
Beyond "modifies a verb, adjective, or other adverb": If a word answers one of the following questions, it is an adverb (adverb phrase or adverbial clause): *When? Where? Why? How? To what extent? How often?* If a word can fit into the following frame, it is an adverb: *Do it____________.*	Eliminate unnecessary adverbs. Choose a verb, adjective, or other adverb that does not need an adverb. Create adverbial phrases and clauses that add detail and sentence variety. **Surface corrections:** Avoid the mistake of using an adjective when an adverb is called for. (*good* and *well*; *bad* and *badly*) Use *fewer* and *less* correctly.
Pronouns	**Content and Style**
Beyond "takes the place of a noun": A pronoun takes the place not only of a noun but of a noun plus all of its modifiers.	Use the most effective point of view for a given writing piece. Clarify who is doing what. **Surface corrections:** Achieve pronoun-antecedent agreement. Use proper pronoun case.
Prepositions	**Content and Style**
Beyond "memorize a list of prepositions": Prepositions, which act adjectivally or adverbially, may be identified using the "anywhere a squirrel can go" device or the "when the squirrel eats breakfast" device	Begin and end sentences in a variety of ways. Add detail and dimension. Open a sentence with a visual. Achieve parallel structure. **Surface corrections:** Achieve subject-verb agreement
Conjunctions	**Content and Style**
Beyond "Conjunction Junction, what's your function?": Favorite coordinating conjunctions: *and, but, so* Favorite subordinating conjunctions: *after, although, as, when, while, unless, until, because, before, if, since*	Establish clear relationships between words, phrases, and clauses within a sentence. Combine sentences to reduce wordiness, strengthen relationships, and create sentence variety. **Surface corrections:** Use proper punctuation between clauses.

If you are an English teacher, I suggest that you begin where you are already comfortable. Work in the context of reading literature and teaching writing through process, and build your grammar-teaching skills over the next two or three years. If the terminology intimidates you, remember that it is you who are intimidated, not the students. Students will absorb technical terms if they are used frequently in context, and with plenty of examples. Teach grammar as a way to improve writing at the revision stage, rather than leaving it to the editing stage: By learning the techniques we've discussed, students can revise their sentences to express more detailed, better organized, and more coherent information.

If you are not an English teacher, you are expected to pay attention to grammar, but not to teach it explicitly. The Checklist for Paragraph Development (Figure 15.2) is an instrument designed to make your life easier by giving students the responsibility of checking over their own work before they hand it in. By using this checklist repeatedly and in multiple classes, students come to understand what is expected of academic writing. (A full-sized version of the checklist is available in Appendix A on page 163.)

Figure 15.2. Checklist for Paragraph Development

I. Structure

☐ 1. Does the first sentence state the point of the paragraph, setting the reader up for the details and conclusion to follow?

☐ 2. Do the middle sentences give details such as reasons, explanations, examples, quotes, and facts?

☐ 3. Does the last sentence help us understand why we should be convinced, *or* why the ideas in the paragraph are important, *or* what is next?

II. Coherence

The sentences in the paragraph should stick together because you have done at least one of these things:

☐ 1. Did you repeat key words?

☐ 2. Do the last few words of each sentence set up the first few words of the next sentence?

☐ 3. Did you tie ideas together with conjunctions such as *and, but, so* and *after, as, although, when, while, until, because, before, if*?

III. Sentence Sense and Style

☐ 1. Is each sentence a complete sentence?

☐ 2. Are you sure that you have no run-on sentences?

☐ 3. Are you sure that you have not used the same word to begin several sentences, especially *and* or *then*?

☐ 4. Are you sure that you have not overused the following words, especially in sentence beginnings: *and, then, there is, there are, there was, there were, it is, it was*?

☐ 5. Have you expanded your vocabulary by using at least one word that you have not used before in writing?

☐ 6. Have you shown respect for the reader by writing neatly, proofreading, and using the kind of "formal school language" that appeals to the reader?

CHAPTER 16

Teaching Vocabulary

About Vocabulary Tiers

In *Bringing Words to Life: Robust Vocabulary Instruction*, Isabel Beck, Margaret G. McKeown, and Linda Kucan (2002) describe a convenient way to divide the English language into three tiers. Their terminology has been adopted by the Common Core.

Tier I consists of the ordinary, common, everyday words of social communication. If we were talking about mountains, the Tier 1 words might be *mountain, high, height, trees, rocks, plants, green, growing*, and other one or two-syllable words that the native speaker of English absorbs in the course of daily life. Those who teach English as a new language to speakers of other languages use the term BICS (Basic Interpersonal Communication Set) to designate these words. Generally, the set of Tier 1 words consists of approximately 2,000 to 3,000 words. A new speaker of English will probably become proficient on the Tier I words in two or three years. We like to think of the Tier I words as "words you knew by the time you were ten years old" or "words you 'just know." Tier I words, despite their casual register, are powerful for writing poetry and other literature, for expressing emotion, and for establishing friendships. Tier I words put English speakers at ease because they are down to earth.

While Tier I words suffice for informal social conversation, academic and business communication draw from a second level of English, and are designated as Tier II. Beck et al. define Tier II as "words that are of high frequency for mature language users and are found across a variety of domains" (Beck, p. 8). In reference to mountains again, we would use words such as *formation, eleva-*

tion, vegetation, ascend, descend, geography, feature, and *development*. It's important to note that Tier II words are not inherently more difficult than Tier I words; they are simply less frequently used in the students' lives. The relative level of what we think of as difficulty is actually our comfort level with a word based on its familiarity in our world of words. A five-year-old who plays with Barbie dolls will know the word *accessories*, a Tier II word. The same child may also know words like *inappropriate, Tyrannosaurus Rex, recycle,* and other multisyllabic words that buzz around her world.

Tier II words tend to have certain features because most of these words are Latin based. That means they have a root—a word component that can appear in slightly different variants used to create a whole family of words. The root *-gress*, for example, often appears as *grad-*. It is used to create a whole array of words having to do with *to step*. From this root, we have *progress* (*progresses, progressed, progressing, progressive, progression*), *grade* (*grades, graded, grading, gradation, gradient*), *degrade* (*degrades, degraded, degrading, degradation*), *retrograde* (*retrogression*), *graduate* (*graduates, graduated, graduating, graduation*), *gradual* (*gradually*), *regress* (*regresses, regressed, regressing, regressive, regression*), and others. It is estimated that 65 percent of English vocabulary derives from Latin (and Greek, and these etymologies blend, so there's not always a clear pedigree of a Tier II word). Whereas the Tier I words do not tend to produce whole branches of related words, the Tier II words are accessible through an understanding of a finite set of key roots, listed below.

In addition to their Latin roots, Tier II words are expandable through the use of various prefixes and suffixes. The prefixes (*in-, un-, re-, de-, ex-,* etc.) change the meaning of the base word, usually creating its opposite. The suffixes (*-able, -ation, -ness, -ment, -ity, -ism, -cious*) transform the base word from one part of speech to another, enabling it to function into a sentence.

Tier III words are the kinds of words you would find in a glossary. These specific technical words are used narrowly. Tier II words usually have a Tier I correspondent (*dead* is Tier I; *deceased*, Tier II; *ask*, Tier I, *question* or *interrogate*, Tier II; *fast* or *quick*, Tier I; *rapid, accelerated*, Tier II). Tier III words, however, do not have correspondents in the other two tiers. Words like *photosyhthesis, molecule, Impressionism, socialism, polysaccharide* must be used as is.

We already teach Tier III vocabulary as part of content, and we do a pretty good job, giving full explanations, examples, visuals, opportunities for use, and meaningful exposure. But we can't spend that kind of explicit teaching time on Tier II words for several reasons. One, we don't have time, and we don't know which of the Tier II words our students do not know. Two, Tier II words are elusive. We assume that somewhere along the line the students already learned or absorbed these words. Three, Tier II words often vary in meaning from one domain to another. Words like *property, value,* and *function* mean something different in English, social studies, math, and science classes. And four, most of the

Tier II words are not learned through definition or even explanation; they are learned through experience. That is, we hear them in use multiple times in different contexts, and we absorb them through natural acquisition.

Immersion in Tier II Vocabulary

For academic success, it is not enough to know the Tier III words because they always appear in the context of Tier II words. Nowhere is this more true than on high-stakes tests, where students can't tackle the questions not because they don't know the information, but because they don't understand the question because of 1) the complex sentences and 2) the Tier II language.

As students look over a list of Tier II words, some will be altogether unfamiliar—complete strangers. Many others are partially known (acquaintances) while others are fully known (friends). Using that paradigm, how do we make the strangers into acquaintances, the acquaintances into friends?

Actually, the answer can be found by considering how the people we know move along the continuum from strangers to acquaintances, and ultimately, to friends. A stranger becomes an acquaintance merely by awareness of that person's identify. Likewise, we become acquainted with a word as soon as it is brought to our unconscious or conscious attention. We've heard of it, albeit we don't know much about it. As with people who are acquaintances, students can take three steps to turn word acquaintances into friends.

1. **Spend time.** This refers, simply enough, to exposure. When we consider the difference between the words students hear in their home and social lives and the words they need to hear in their academic lives, we get an idea of how important it is for us to expose students to Tier II and III words.

2. **Get to know the inside.** We know the inside of words when we know their Latin and Greek roots

3. **Have fun.** This is where the games and puzzles come in. Games and puzzles are the best way (next to habitual reading) to develop flexibility about word meanings. Games and puzzles also provide a platform for repeated exposure to meanings, forms, and spelling.

Word Study for Tier II Vocabulary

The term *word study* is associated with the *reader's workshop* teaching framework. Content-area teachers, grades 6–12, may not be familiar with either of these terms except in a generic sense, as both reader's workshop and word study have traditionally been limited to elementary education. However, the kind of word study done in a reader's workshop can be highly effective for learning the technical language (aka Tier III words) of science, social studies, and technical subjects on the secondary level.

In this context, word study involves much more than just learning a single word by its textbook or glossary definition. Word study refers to the practice of coming to understand how words are related to other words having similar structure and, therefore, meaning. Word study involves learning words thoroughly, acquiring the linguistic information that demystifies the rare, specific, and multisyllabic words that characterize learning about technical subjects. Because it is just these words that intimidate students and impede reading fluency, word study promises to improve a student's full performance in the content areas.

The heart of word study is noticing the patterns of how words are constructed. What letter combinations do sets of words about the same thing have in common? For example, if we look at the list of elements in the periodic table, we notice lots of patterns that are quite significant in unlocking the meaning of Tier III science words, as we will see on the next page. All we need to do is ask students to look over the names of the 118 known elements and ask them to observe and report. (Reporting on observations is a key behavior in science anyway) We want students to work together so that they both say and hear the words naming the elements, many of which are strange indeed.

Discoveries about word structures in a given set of Tier III words may be displayed in a *semantic features chart*, as shown in Figure 16.1. A reproducible version of this chart is available in Appendix D on page 173.

Figure 16.1. Semantic Features Chart

SEMANTIC FEATURES CHART **Common Word Endings of the Elements**				
-ium	**-on**	**-gen**	**-ine**	**-y**
helium, lithium, beryllium, sodium, magnesium, potassium, calcium, scandium, titanium, vanadium, chromium, gallium, germanium, selenium, rubidium, strontium, yttrium, zirconium, niobium, technetium, ruthenium, rhodium, palladium, cadmium, indium, tellurium, cesium, barium, cerium, praseodymium, neodymium, promethium, samarium, europium, gadolinium, terbium, dysprosium, holmium, erbium, thulium, ytterbium, lutetium, hafnium, rhenium, osmium, iridium, thallium, polonium, francium, radium, actinium, thorium, protactinium, uranium, neptunium, plutonium, americium, curium, berkelium, californium, einsteinium, fermium, mendelevium, nobelium, lawrencium, rutherfordium, dubinium, seaborgium, borhium, hassium, meiterium, darmstadium, roetgenium, copernicium, ununtrium, ununquadium, ununpentium, ununhexium, unundeptium, ununcoctium	boron, carbon, neon, silicon, argon, iron, krypton, xenon, radon	hydrogen, nitrogen, oxygen	fluorine, chlorine, bromine, iodine, astatine	antimony, mercury **other:** sulfur, cobalt, nickel, copper, zinc, arsenic, silver, tin, lead, platinum, gold, bismuth, aluminum

The value of such a chart is that it gets students looking at words analytically, enabling them to break down some very complicated words in terms of their units of meaning (morphemes).

Word sorts are a common word-study activity in which we take a group of words related by meaning, structure, or grammatical features and categorize them accordingly into subsets. The word sort can be based on meaning (gathering words related to the same topic), structure (prefix-root-suffix), or grammatical features (singular/plural; parts of speech). Word sorts are worth the time it takes to do them because they reinforce learning in the following ways:

- **Student engagement.** Word sorts are fun. The human brain loves finding patterns. Patterns make the world come together and make sense.
- **Accessibility.** Word sorts are not supposed to be difficult or frustrating. Yet, the engagement of doing a word sort helps the learner group like items. Grouping facilitates memory, understanding, and retrieval.
- **Social context.** As students work together, they build familiarity with Tier III words that are new and strange sounding.
- **Meaning.** The most valuable result of word sorting is that finding patterns and grouping words with common features brings out the meaning of whole words and word components.

Word Study Is Better Than Mnemonics

Word sorts are a better aid to memory than mnemonic devices, such as acronyms, rhymes, and jingles because word sorts rely upon meaning and/or structure as an organizing principle. Sometimes, the items in a set need to be memorized through a mnemonic device because there's no meaning-grounded way to connect them. An example would be the order of the planets learned through the famous acronym *My very educated mother just served us nine plums* (alternatively, … *just served us nachos*, if we expel Pluto from the solar system). Little harm is done, and convenience is achieved, by remembering the five Great Lakes with the acronym HOMES (Huron, Ontario, Michigan, Erie, Superior). But we should resort to mnemonic devices only after we've determined that a more meaning-based, illuminating connection cannot be found. We should play to that part of the brain that remembers relationships because they make inherent sense.

Teachers and students get excited about mnemonic devices. They are fun and effective, but their effectiveness is shallow compared to the meaning-based approach. Mnemonics facilitate recall of facts without linking to an understanding of concepts. Also, a mnemonic can be forgotten. We may remember the device, but not the information that it was invented to represent. Word study *does* lead to the understanding of concepts because true and deep meanings can be discovered through an examination of words sharing the same components. Teaching mnemonics may help students come up with other mnemonics, but teaching them word components will help them achieve the higher level thinking of making informed guesses about new words.

Think about information that you want students to memorize. Try to find meaning-based word-study activities to replace—or at least undergird mnemonic devices that you and they may have relied on in the past. When information is understood first, memorization is easier and more advisable. Think, for example, about the need to know significant dates in history. No history teacher would discount the importance of knowing when significant events and developments occurred *relative to other events and developments* to get a sense of historical trends. Yet, if all we know about history how to do a matching column of years and events, if all we can do is recite state capitals, if all we can do is identify countries by their shapes, then we can hardly be said to know history or geography.

Word Study Is Also Phrase Study

Inasmuch as phrases constitute single units of meaning, the brain can process phases as single words. When two or more words are paired together enough, they eventually meld as one word, a compound word, such as the first word in this paragraph. In academic discourse, there are lots of phrases that appear repeatedly and always mean the same specific thing. The brain loves to conserve its energy by simplifying, shortcutting to the expected message. In this way, familiar information clusters (patterns) are processed together rather than broken down. For lack of a better term, we will call these information clusters *academic flash phrases*. We need to make our students recognize them instantaneously, as if they are a single word.

An example of an academic flash phrase in the field of mathematics is the phrase *frequency distribution*. We actually have five units of meaning here: The base word *frequent*, an adjective, is morphed into a noun (*-cy*) but the brain of the statistician processes it as a noun instantaneously because of familiarity. The base word *distribute*, a verb, is morphed into a noun (*-tion*), also processed instantly. But, in addition to being able to process these individual words instantly, she has the ability to process the phrase *frequency distribution* without having to break the phrase down into its components. *Frequency distribution* is processed as a single word because these words are together a lot.

There is an endless list of academic flash phrases, but you won't find them in novels and poems, where the language is much more varied than language found in technical discourse.

Ironically, perhaps, the Tier III words give us less to worry about than the Tier II words. While we teach Tier III words explicitly and well, we make false assumptions about the extent to which students already know or have the capability to learn Tier II words. My experience in working with teachers at elementary and secondary levels is that, when shown a list of generic Tier II words that appear with great frequency in academic text, secondary teachers insist that students should have "come to them" already knowing such words, while the elementary folks bristle that these words are "too hard for elementary children." Of course, the fact is that anyone can learn any word if that word is used frequently enough with enough helpful context surrounding it.

How Words Get Learned and Stay Learned

Academic vocabulary undergirds all of the Standards. In fact, it undergirds all academic learning—arguably, all learning. "Words are not just words," says Marilyn Jager Adams (as cited in the Common Core State Standards, p. 32). "They are the nexus—the interface—between communication and thought." Words afford understanding. The understanding that words afford is applicable not only to interpersonal communication, but to thought itself. Words formulate thought, whether the thought turns into speech/writing or not.

This section discusses how words get (and do not get) learned and stay learned, the different kinds of vocabulary instruction (explicit and implicit), and authentic assessment (formative and summative), for vocabulary growth.

How Words Do *Not* Get Learned and Stay Learned

Despite the strong connection among a student's vocabulary and reading comprehension and overall academic achievement, "vocabulary instruction has been neither frequent nor systematic in most schools" (Common Core Appendix A, p. 32).

Let's look at a very common way that vocabulary is approached in middle and high schools. A ninth-grade student, we'll call her Olivia, is given a write-in vocabulary workbook at the beginning of the school year. The workbook contains some twenty-five units, each introducing twenty *unrelated* words presented in *no context*. The workbook provides a variety of types of information about each word: diacritical markings for pronunciation, part of speech, a brief definition, use of the word in a substantial sentence, and a few synonyms and antonyms.

Mondays in Olivia's English language arts class always begin with a fifteen minute vocabulary lesson that consists of round-robin reading of the twenty words, their definitions, and the sentence in the workbook. Very little, if any, further information is given about each word to supplement what is in the workbook. After students read the words, they are given about seven minutes to do some of the fill-in-the-blank exercises: sentence completions; matching the words on the list to a phrase in which a synonym is boldfaced, then doing the same for antonyms; selecting the correct word in context from a choice of two words, and reading an informational passage in which the words are used in context; followed by three multiple-choice questions. It takes Olivia 45 minutes to an hour to complete these exercises. She is to do this for homework or when there are leftover minutes in class during the week. On Friday, there is a quiz on these words. The quiz duplicates one of the exercises, and this format provides Olivia with motivation to do the exercises herself. Should she need more support, there's an online resource to go along with the workbook. It pronounces the words and reads the sentences aloud. All in all, it's a pretty mundane affair, but Olivia does it without complaint or contemplation as just one of those things you do in school. When Olivia's parents went to school, they used the same workbook.

The words are mostly Latin based (Tier II), the kind of words found in literature. Olivia considers these words that "smart people" would know, and she duly admires those who use them. Her friends don't use these words. These are the words on an SAT or ACT exam in the vocabulary or reading-comprehension sections, words like *abhor, bellicose, castigate, demure, exigent, flout, grimace, haughty, illicit, jape, knavery, laudable, martial, noxious, ossify, placate, querulous, restive, satiate, terse, usury, vitiate, winsome, xenophobe,* and *zeal*. These are exactly the kinds of words Olivia would expect to see on a vocabulary list. She happens to know one or two of them cold (*illicit, haughty*); a few others she would be able to recognize if used in a familiar context. She's familiar with the saying "Nature abhors a vacuum," and she can figure out what *abhor* means in that context. She can also figure out the contextual meaning of *flout*, as in *to flout the rules*. She knows what *martial arts* means, and she's heard of *martial law*, which she knows is something that is invoked when street violence gets out of control, even though she's never really connected *martial law* to *martial arts*. But, she is not reminded of these familiarities, so she doesn't bring them into her awareness as she's memorizing definitions.

Several of the words can be connected to words Olivia knows: *bellicose-belligerent, laudable-applaud, noxious-obnoxious, querulous-quarrel, satiate-satisfy-saturate, illicit-license*. And there are a few more subtle connections based on etymology. *Abhor*, for example, consists of two known word components: *ab*, meaning "away" (*abnormal, abstract*) and *hor*, meaning "to tremble" (*horrid, horrible*). The word *martial* is related to *Mars*, whom Olivia knows is the Roman god of war.

Most of the words do not connect to what she is learning in other classes, or, if they do (*xenophobe, bellicose, usury, ossify*), the connection is not brought to her attention, so she doesn't realize it. At least one of the words, *ossify*, could become more memorable if associated with a striking visual, such as a photograph of an ossuary sculpture of a chandelier made of human bones! Another of the words, *restive*, is counterintuitive. Instead of meaning "restful," it means the opposite, "restless." So Olivia is not only steered away from using her prior knowledge, she is actually encouraged to mistrust it. Her teacher warns, "Restive means 'agitated, impatient,' it does not mean what you think it means. It's a tricky one." The teacher's explanation reinforces Olivia's suspicion that vocabulary words are meant to trip you up, to lure you into the trap of using your linguistic intuition, only to punish you on the test for not doing the "right" thing: memorizing the definition. Be careful of words like *restive*. She will asterisk that one on her workbook page.

Some of the words are used mainly or exclusively in very narrow fields, giving us little opportunity to use them in speech and writing (although we do encounter them while reading in the fields in which they are used). *Knavery*, for example, a word meaning "disreputable or untrustworthy actions," is seldom used outside of Shakespearean text, although it's a charming word. The word *vitiate* is used almost exclusively in the legal field, referring to the annulment of a contractual agreement. Yet, Olivia and her classmates are learning these words for the quiz just the same as if they were words that are much more common in conversation and literature.

Words have nuance, connotation, collocation (other words that tend to go with them), register (level of formality), and various forms, and they can even be adapted to various parts of speech. None of this information about words is included in Olivia's teacher's methodology, which is essentially to leave the students alone with the exercises, administer the weekly quiz, and move on.

The exercises themselves provide some processing of the words. It would be better, however, if the exercises were done with a partner, as part of the life of the class, rather than alone as homework. Even when we assume that the students will be making agreements to lessen the workload by parceling out the exercises and copying the filled-in answers from each other, there's still some value in the exercises, as they do offer meaningful context that gets the students thinking about the meaning of the words and how they fit into a sentence or phrase. (The teacher does occasionally spot-check the workbooks but gives them only the most cursory evaluation to see if the blanks are filled in enough that it looks as if students have done their homework. Many students in Olivia's class fill in the words at random.)

Olivia's teacher herself seldom uses the words on the vocabulary list in class. It is as if these words belong somewhere outside the natural corpus of words that a real person would actually use to communicate. When a word does pop up, either in readings or in (the teacher's) speech, students like Olivia perk up a little and acknowledge it. "Ooh! A vocabulary word! How about that?" The very term *vocabulary word* as opposed to just *vocabulary* or *word*, for that matter, betrays the benchwarmer status to which these words are consigned. Like fancy sample bottles of perfume that contain only water, *vocabulary words* are for display only. Like pinned butterflies, they don't take wing.

Now let's look at another model that is considered to be better—but it isn't by much, really. Many teachers extract vocabulary words from the literature that the students are reading. A vocabulary list from George Orwell's *Animal Farm* might look like this: *inscribe, harvest, ensconce, pasture, knoll, orchard, quarry, huddle, chaff, gambol, windfall, assemble, superannuated, cryptic, maxim, readjustment, unalterable, formulate, piebald, ignominious, disinter, collaborate, tureen, swill, decree, slag, procure, clime, capitulate, mincing, whelp, tractable, cog,* and on and on. A list like this has the advantage of at least being classifiable into some grouping relevant to the story, in this case, farm life. But there are too many words to be learned in a meaningful way, many of them will be encountered only once in the text, and, looked at as a whole, comprise a random collection of unrelated, decontextualized words not much different from those in the workbook units. Factoring in the lack of exercises available to process the words, as in the workbook model, the "words taken from literature" model is not likely to result in more true vocabulary learning than the workbook. Unless the words are taught deeply in terms of their meaning in the novel (such as why the author chose these particular words over similar ones, how the diction affects the reader, the tone and poetic value of particular words), deriving a lengthy list of words that students probably don't know from assigned literature is probably not going to result in true growth. Context alone is notoriously unhelpful. The chance of being able to figure out the meaning of a word in a single context is only 10–15 percent, and that is for a very good reason: An author chooses the best words for the intended message and assumes that the reader is familiar with the words he or she chooses. It takes multiple exposures to a word and its various forms to derive its array of meanings. It is estimated that a reader who is reading at his or her instructional level (meaning that 95 percent of the words are known to the reader) will harvest one word for every twenty paragraphs. And that is assuming that the word is repeated.

What kind of learner is Olivia becoming as a result of this vocabulary instruction? She's becoming a memorizer of definitions of words in a single form. She's becoming a student who equates learning with producing correct, finite answers on a predictable test that requires the shallowest of knowledge (brief definitions) of a bunch of words. She's becoming a learner adept at hitting the reset button in her brain every Monday, drawing in this week's batch of twenty words, as last week's batch are cleared away until they are temporarily encored for the "unit test" at the end of each quarter. She's becoming the kind of learner whose only questions about words are "Are these words on the test?" "Are these the definitions that are going to be used on the test?" "Is this the order the words will be given on the test?" Perhaps worst of all, she is becoming the kind of learner who thinks this is learning.

What she's not becoming is better at vocabulary. Not only does she clear her head of the words right after the quiz, and not only does she not use the words she's learned in her speech or writing, but she's learned nothing about words! She hasn't learned that words have components, families, forms, nuances, connotations, register, backstories. She hasn't learned that the spelling of a word can reveal clues to its meaning, that synonyms can't be used willy-nilly as replacements any more than shoes of the same size can look fine with any outfit. She's not learning that words have collocations (other words that tend to go with them) or how etymology illuminates meaning. Most importantly, Olivia is not learning how to use her own language intuition, curiosity, and sense of fun to grow her vocabulary.

It is not that it is impossible to nurture genuine vocabulary growth through a workbook or literature-based paradigm. It is possible to do an excellent job of vocabulary teaching if the teacher applies key principles of language acquisition. What follows are a few of these key principles and their instructional implications.

- **Repeated Exposure/Rich Context.** Most words are absorbed through repeated exposure in a rich context. Show me a four-year-old whose parent is a teacher, and I'll show you a four-year-old who knows the word *inappropriate*. Show me a first-grader whose teacher has recently been to a workshop, and I'll show you a first-grader who knows the phrase *graphic organizer*. Looked at this way, we understand that there is no such thing as a difficult word, only an infrequent word. Language-acquisition expert Stephen Krashen (www.sdkrashen.com) coined the term *comprehensible input* to capture the principle that if we know enough of the context, and if we want to understand the message, we can figure out unknown words, especially when they are repeated. The instructional implication of the comprehensible input principle is that educators have to think about the level of language that they use to speak to students and the extent to which students are reading. Teachers need to develop the *teacherly habit* of using words that students need to know and nestling those words in enough comprehensible input that students can figure them out in context. Tier III words are taught explicitly, but Tier II words need to be heard naturally, often, and in their various forms. Let's come back to Olivia for a moment. When Olivia was a toddler, her parents spoke to her using words they knew she didn't know, but there was a context. "Are you thirsty? Would you like some juice? Would you like the yellow juice or the purple juice?" This conversation was supported by visuals, facial expressions, and gestures. It was prompted by a need to communicate with Olivia. Krashen talks about speaking using vocabulary that is "just beyond" what students already know. That is how babies, toddlers, and kindergartners learn new words. *In fact, that is how everyone learns new words throughout life.*

- **Opportunities for Meaningful Use.** By meaningful use, we don't mean a matching column, a fill-in exercise, or the on-demand production of a sentence that uses the new word. The instructional implication of the *meaningful use* principle is applied when students are given a word bank consisting of words that are aligned to a specific writing or speaking experience: "It's the perfect opportunity to use these new words; now go ahead and use them." Cooperative learning rich in content and purpose, like a science lab, offers opportunities for meaningful use. When my students did small-group book talks, I (Amy) would write a handful of what I would call "literature-talking words" on the board to encourage their use in the book talks. When students talked "around" these words, I'd translate, using Tier II and III words.

- **Lots of Free Voluntary Reading.** Arguably, reading is the best way to grow vocabulary after the age of eight or nine. Definitely, reading will take place more if the reading is fun and without pressure. The instructional implication is that students must have access to reading material that is interesting to them, and they must be given time during the school day to kick back and read paper texts or the Internet. Even reading about the same subject all the time will improve vocabulary because the reader, accumulating substantial background knowledge, will develop the ability to read more complex text about their topics of interest. They will have repeated exposure to the set of vocabulary words that are used in those topics of interest. Stephen Krashen calls this "the case for narrow reading." Krashen has found that better readers do read series of books by the same author and on the same topic.

- **Fun and Games.** Word games and puzzles foster mental flexibility, reinforce spelling patterns, create a positive environment for learning words, and provide practice in stretching word meanings. Krashen speaks of the brain's affective filter, a protective mechanism that causes the learner to shut down language acquisition when the learner feels discouraged, threatened, or inhibited. Word games, be they social or solitary, reduce stress for those who enjoy them. Another way of using fun as a word-learning tool is Total Physical Response and Storytelling

(TPRS). Developed by Blaine Ray, TPRS is a highly engaging method for second-language acquisition in which students use gesture, movement, and repeated questions to tell and understand a story. The instructional implication of this principle is that teachers need to lose their inhibitions about using games, puzzles, skits, physicality, and storytelling in class as part of a legitimate, research-based method for growing vocabulary in Tier II and III language.

- **Well-Planned Explicit Instruction on Useful Words.** On average, students can be expected to learn and keep approximately 400 words per year through explicit instruction, assuming that the explicit instruction is done well. Effective explicit instruction on wisely selected words, then, does have significant impact and is worth doing. There are three instructional implications. First, how do we select words worthy of the time it takes to instruct explicitly? Second, what does effective explicit instruction look like? Third, where do Latin and Greek word components fit in, what are the most useful ones, and how are these best taught? I suggest three criteria for selecting a word for explicit instruction. First is the usefulness of the word. Is this a Tier III word that students must know to learn the content? Is this, perhaps, a word that is fairly infrequent in casual conversation, but educated people are expected to know it? The second criterion has to do with return on investment. To what extent can I use this word to leverage my way into other words I'd like students to know? For example, if I teach a word with a Latin or Greek word root or prefix, I can parlay that into other words having that component. A word I'd like to teach may have numerous synonyms and antonyms and, while we're in the neighborhood, we can visit those words as well. Third, am I enthusiastic about this word? Might I have a story or two where this word comes in handy? It's important that word instruction be animated, meaningful, satisfying, and even humorous. Teaching words deeply involves teaching all known aspects of a word, way beyond its dictionary definition. Semantic maps, also called word maps, display various features of a word at a glance. For examples of word maps on general vocabulary, visit my website, www.amybenjamin.com. To teach from a word map, I would elaborate on each of its sections and have the students handwrite the map as I explain it. Ideally, students should be able to create and explain their own word maps.

- **Distributed Practice.** If you think about your efforts to learn students' names at the beginning of the school year, you will recognize the principle of distributed practice. Do you know the names of all of your students at the end of the first day? (If you do, ask yourself how you would do if they all sat in a different place on Day Two!) Chances are, you need to hear their names several times over several days. Repetition over time is what embeds learning. The instructional implication is that vocabulary growth, incremental and cumulative, happens slowly but surely. The weekly vocabulary test followed by no further exposure to the word tells us nothing about vocabulary growth, as we explore below.

Authentic Assessment for Vocabulary Growth

Vocabulary learning should be permanent. If words are washed away after the quiz, there is no point in learning them. Studying for a vocabulary test is valuable only if the student is going to remember the words after the test. So, an announced and expected vocabulary test does not give us information about whether the word has actually taken its place in the mind of the learner.

Only unannounced vocabulary assessments give us the truth about vocabulary retention. We can't assess aural or oral vocabulary. We can assess a student's written vocabulary by asking to what extent the use of Tier II and III words in the student's writing is growing.

Authentic assessment for vocabulary growth is not as easy as the weekly vocabulary quiz. Authentic assessment involves contextualized use, and not all of the words that students have learned in a given period of time are going to be used. A student may know a word but use it in a context that suggests only partial knowledge. Knowing a word is not an all-or-nothing thing.

Assessment for vocabulary is not straightforward. It is certainly not a matter of giving a multiple-choice or matching test for a word list. Shallow word knowledge, defined as the ability to pick out a definition that appears amid other definitions, is not the only indicator of a student's vocabulary development.

For vocabulary assessment to be authentic and informative, we need to make it ongoing, requiring the cumulative and sustained use of words that are new to the student's productive vocabulary. We need both formative and summative assessments for vocabulary that consider a student's vocabulary growth and the student's ability to use strategies to confront unfamiliar words.

The Academic Word List and How to Use It

Picture four hundred different college-level textbooks representing a variety of fields. Think about the words that would be in these textbooks, which would each have the Tier III words specific to its own subject areas. But what Tier II words would they have in common? Which of those Tier II words would appear most often? Now picture your students. To what extent would they know the Tier II words thoroughly enough to be able to comprehend how the Tier III words are used in those college textbooks? And, most importantly, what are the Tier II words that appear most commonly and pervasively in college-level textbooks?

The Academic Word List (AWL), developed in 2000 by Averil Coxhead, is a compilation of 570 word families (by "word family," we mean base words, the simplest form of the word, to which suffixes and prefixes may be added). It has been shown that these word families account for approximately 10 percent of the words in college textbooks and other readings (p. 6). The Academic Word List is your one-stop shopping for the Tier II words that your students absolutely must know and use for both reading and writing academically and in business.

The Academic Word List is organized into ten subsets. The words in each subset are arranged alphabetically, but the subsets themselves, 1 through 10, are arranged according to their degree of frequency in academic text books. Therefore, the words on the earlier subsets are higher priority because these are more frequent than the words on the last few. You will find that your particular students already know at least something about many of the words on the Academic Word List, especially on the first few subsets. But you will also find that many of your students need work on this list. Furthermore, you will (probably) find that these are not the words that are usually on vocabulary lists for students to learn, even though we admit that many students do not know them thoroughly.

Coming to know and appreciate the Academic Word List is an important step forward for a school. Everyone who interacts with students should be aware of the Academic Word List and should enrich his or her speech with these words whenever possible. Most of the words on the Academic Word List are learned through implicit instruction: constant repetition in a meaningful context. Some may need to be taught explicitly. However, explicit instruction on these words will not take the place of steady exposure in a meaningful, domain-specific context. Most of the words carry a broad definition which narrows in the context of a particular subject. For example, the word *define* (Subset 1) means "explain the meaning of" in English, social studies, science, and mathematics, but when the physical education teacher speaks of *defining your biceps* through weight-lifting, she doesn't mean "tell me in words what biceps are." When the interior design teacher instructs students to use architectural flourishes to *define a space*, he isn't looking for a written definition of what a formal dining area is. Most of the words on the Academic Word List are flexible like this.

In addition to the (limited) explicit instruction and pervasive exposure, the words on the Academic Word List can be reinforced through games. On my website (www.amybenjamin.com) you will find various word games, categorized by subsets. If you want exercises where the words are given in various forms and contexts, you may find them at www.lextutor.ca/concordances/sentences and www.dcielts.com/ielts-vocabulary/awl-exercises.

Figure 16.2 shows Averil Coxhead's Academic Word List, modified slightly. It is also available in Appendix C on page 169.

Figure 16.2. Coxhead's Academic Word List

Subset 1: analyze, approach, area, assess, assume, authority, available, benefit, concept, consist, context, constitute, contract, data, define, derive, distribute, economy, environment, establish, estimate, evident, factor, finance, formula, function, income, indicate, individual, interpret, involve, issue, labor, legal, legislate, method, occur, percent, period, principle, proceed, process, policy, require, research, respond, role, section, sector, significant, source, specific, structure, theory, vary

Subset 2: achieve, acquire, administrate, affect, appropriate, aspect, assist, category, commission, complex, conduct, consequent, construct, consume, credit, culture, design, distinct, element, evaluate, feature, impact, institute, invest, maintain, obtain, perceive, positive, potential, previous, primary, range, region, regulate, relevant, reside, resource, restrict, secure, select, site, strategy, survey, tradition, transfer

Subset 3: alternative, circumstance, comment, compensate, component, consent, considerable, constant, constrain, contribute, convene, coordinate, core, corporate, correspond, criteria, deduce, demonstrate, document, dominate, emphasis, ensure, exclude, find, framework, illustrate, immigrate, imply, initial, instance, interact, justify, layer, link, maximize, negate, outcome, philosophy, physical, proportion, publish, react, register, rely, scheme, sequence, shift, specify, sufficient, technical, technique, valid, volume

Subset 4: access, adequacy, annual, apparent, approximate, attitude, attribute, civil, code, commit, concentrate, confer, contrast, cycle, debate, despite, dimension, domestic, emerge, ethnic, grant, hence, hypothesis, implement, implicate, impose, integrate, internal, investigate, mechanism, occupy, option, output, overall, parallel, parameter, phrase, prior, principal, professional, project, promote, regime, resolve, retain, series, statistic, status, stress, subsequent, undertake

Subset 5: academy, adjust, alter, amend, capacity, clause, compound, consult, decline, discrete, enable, energy, enforce, entity, equivalent, evolve, expand, expose, external, facilitate, fundamental, generate, liberal, license, logic, margin, modify, monitor, network, notion, objective, orient, perspective, precise, prime, psychology, pursue, ratio, reject, revenue, stable, style, substitute, sustain, symbol, target, transit, trend, version, welfare, whereas

Subset 6: abstract, acknowledge, accuracy, aggregate, allocate, assign, bond, capable, cite, cooperate, discriminate, display, diverse, domain, edit, enhance, estate, exceed, explicit, federal, fee, flexible, furthermore, gender, incentive, incorporate, incidence, index, inhibit, initiate, input, interval, mitigate, minimum, ministry, motive, neutral, nevertheless, overseas, precede, presume, rational, recover, reveal, scope, subsidy, trace, transform, underlie, utilize

Subset 7: adapt, advocate, channel, classic, comprehensive, comprise, confirm, contrary, convert, decade, deny, differentiate, dispose, dynamic, equip, eliminate, empirical, extract, finite, foundation, gradient, guarantee, hierarchy, identical, ideology, infer, innovate, insert, intervene, isolate, media, mode, paradigm, phenomenon, priority, prohibit, publication, quote, release, reverse simulate, sole, somewhat, submit, successor, thesis, transmit, ultimate, unique, voluntary

Subset 8: abandon, accompany, accumulate, ambiguous, appendix, appreciate, arbitrary, automate, bias, chart, clarify, commodity, complement, conform, contemporary, contradict, crucial, currency, denote, detect, deviate, displace, eventual, exhibit, exploit, fluctuate, guideline, implicit, induce, inevitable, infrastructure, inspect, intense, manipulate, minimize, nuclear, offset, predominant, prospect, radical, reinforce, restore, revise, tension, terminate, theme, thereby, uniform, vehicle, via, virtual, widespread

Subset 9: accommodate, analogy, anticipate, assure, attain, behalf, cease, coherent, coincide, commence, compatible, concurrent, confine, controversy, converse, device, devote, diminish, distort, duration, erode, ethic, found, format, inherent, insight, integral, intermediate, manual, mature, mediate, medium, military, minimal, mutual, norm, overlap, passive, portion, preliminary, protocol, qualitative, refine, restrain, revolution, rigid, route, scenario, sphere, subordinate, supplement, suspend, trigger, unify, violate

Subset 10: adjacent, albeit, assemble, collapse, colleague, compile, conceive, convince, depress, encounter, forthcoming, incline, integrity, intrinsic, invoke, levy, likewise, nonetheless, notwithstanding, ongoing, panel, persist, pose, reluctance, so-called, straightforward, undergo, whereby

Latin Word Roots

Eighty percent of the words on the Academic Word List come from Latin and Greek word components. (This puts students who speak Spanish, French, Italian, Portuguese, or Romanian at a big advantage because of the cognates.) Lists of Latin word roots are easy enough to find, but we can't just hand students a list of roots to memorize.

"Word Root of the Day" is one good model, especially when we present students with a short list of related words at least one of which they already know. For example, in Subset 4, we find the word *access*, which grows from the root *-cess*, meaning "to yield." Students already know the words *necessary, success,* and *excess*. We can add *cessation, incessant* (both derived from *cease*); *succession, successive* (and how they differ from *success*); *process, procession*. We want students to do more than memorize words and definitions; we want them to learn about words and how they begin with a Latin root, which can change and produce offshoots, some of which maintain the meaning of the root, while others wander off like children who grow up and move far away but come home for Christmas.

Figure 16.3 shows a game-like activity that fosters word profusion and deep understandings about Latin roots and how they generate word clusters. The rules are simple. Ask students to work in teams to compile a list of (at least) 100 words that combine prefixes with roots. It's important to use this particular list because students can combine the components into words without having to change any spelling. Just push the prefix and the root together to form a word.

Figure 16.3. The Power 100-Word Challenge

Combine the prefixes with the word roots to create 100 words.
Use only these prefixes and roots. Do not add any letters.

Prefixes	Roots
a-, ab-, ap-, at, co-, com-, con-, de-, di-, dis-, e-, ex-, im-, in-, ob-, op-, per-, pre-, pro-, re-, retro-, sub-, sup-, trans-	-cess, -ceive, clude, -duce, -fer, -gress, -ject -mit,-pel, -plicate, -ply, -port, -pose -scribe, -scription -sist, -solve, -spect, -strict, -struction, -tain, -tract, -verse, -vert, -volve

Suggested Answers:

abcess	devolve	instruction	reduce
abject	digress	inverse	refer
apply	dispel	invert	repel
ascribe	dispose (Subset 7)	involve (Subset 1)	replicate
aspect (Subset 2)	dissolve	object (Subset 5)	reply
attain (Subset 9)	distract	obstruction	report
attract	diverse (Subset 7)	obtain	repose
avert	divert	obverse	resist
commit (Subset 4)	egress	oppose	resolve (Subset 4)
conceive (Subset 10)	eject	perceive (Subset 2)	restrict (Subset 2)
conclude	emit	permit	retain (Subset 4)
confer	evolve (Subset 5)	persist (Subset 10)	retract
congress	excess	pertain	retrospect
construction (Subset 2)	exclude (Subset 3)	perverse	reverse (Subset 7)
contain	expel	pervert	revert
contract (Subset 1)	explicate	preclude	revolve
convert (Subset 7)	extract (Subset 7)	prefer	subject
covert	impel	prescribe	submit (Subset 7)
deceive	implicate (Subset 4)	prescription	subscribe
deduce (Subset 3)	imply (Subset 3)	process (Subset 1)	subscription
defer	import	produce	subsist
deject	impose (Subset 4)	progress	subtract
deport	include	project (Subset 4)	subvert
depose (Subset 7)	induce (Subset 8)	propel	supplicate
describe	infer (Subset 7)	propose	supply
description	inject	prospect (Subset 8)	support
desist	inscribe	protract	transcribe
destruction	inscription	receive	transfer (Subset 2)
detain	insist	recess	transgress
detract	inspect (Subset 8)		transmit (Subset 7)
			transport
			transcription

CHAPTER 17

Spelling as Word Study

Common Core Standard for Language

> **Standard 2: Demonstrates command of the conventions of standard English capitalization, punctuation *and spelling* when writing [emphasis added].**

This segment is not about how to teach spelling in general. It is about how to incorporate very short explanations of spelling (micro-lessons) into your instruction of Tier III words. We'll talk first about the state of spelling instruction that brings students to you with so few and unreliable skills and strategies for spelling complex words. We'll explain a paradigm for understanding how spelling is a thinking activity calling upon multiple cognitive processes. Then we'll offer specific suggestions for the micro-lesson.

Let's begin by establishing the difference between implicit and explicit spelling instruction. Implicit spelling instruction is simply reading. By reading, we pick up *most* of the spelling patterns in the English language. You are familiar with the sense that a written word "looks" right or wrong. You know that certain letter combinations are often seen, rarely seen, or never seen in the English language. By posting readable materials around your classroom, including word walls and notes on the board as you teach, you are reinforcing those visual imprints that result in correct spelling, not only of those words but of others that share their patterns (common and predictable letter combinations).

Implicit instruction (reading) does not teach all words. There is a gap of words that need to be taught explicitly. Explicit teaching involves building awareness of rules, such as the rules of adding prefixes and suffixes. It also involves teaching students to associate certain groups of words with each other so as to cluster similarly spelled words. Association (clustering) of related items is a very effective way of learning, as the brain consolidates individual items into clusters, resulting in efficient retrieval of the individual words. It involves addressing words that are confused with other words, such as homophones, or words whose pronunciation leads to common misspelling. And it involves teaching mnemonics (gimmicks that help us remember but that are themselves forgettable and that do not connect spelling to meaning or patterns). Very few words, *colonel* being one example, need to be taught as true "singletons."

Explicit spelling instruction becomes scarcer and scarcer as we go up the grades, even though students in the upper grades are obviously not finished learning about spelling. Relying on spell-checking devices will get you only so far, as anyone who has ever read a report, as I (Amy) have, on a book titled *Willie Wonka and the Cholera Factory,* will attest. Some students know so little about spelling a target word that either they can't select from the choices offered or their attempt is so far off that the spell-checking device doesn't even know what the desired word is supposed to be.

It is the English language arts teachers at *all* grade levels who are expected to make students proficient spellers to the point where they have credibility in academic or professional situations. It would be unreasonable to expect social studies and science teachers to deliver explicit instruction on Tier I (conversational words) and Tier II (general academic words). Teachers in subjects other than English language arts, however, are responsible for making students proficient spellers on those Tier III words that are part and parcel of the language and learning in *their* subject areas.

Consider the spelling of the following words: *tyranny, theocracy, Byzantine, meiosis, pancreas, quadratic, thermonuclear, oxygenated, neoclassicism, Impressionism,* and *euphonium*. Or even *racism, factor, linear, satellite,* and *theory*. While some of these words may have been introduced in previous years, and while some of them are used in more than one subject area, most of these words are specific to a particular class, and the teacher of that class would be the best person to explicitly teach the spelling along with, and related to, the meaning. Spelling of Tier III words should be taught in the context of word study or linguistic knowledge.

How *Not* to Teach Spelling: Memorization of Random Words

I tutor a sixth-grader whom we will call Andrew. I help him with his English homework, and that includes a weekly spelling list. His teacher derives the spelling words from various content areas, and last week, Andrew had to learn how to spell twenty words related to the science curriculum. The words were *science, temperature, weather, cumulative, nimbus, stratus, atmosphere, pressure, barometer, meteorology, forecast, prediction, observatory, precipitation, sleet, climate, blizzard, thunder, lightning*, and *instruments*.

Andrew was told to learn his words by practicing them, which meant using a procedure that applied to every spelling list (like this one) every week: "Look at the word. Say the word. Spell the word aloud while looking at if you have to. Write the word three times. Spell the word aloud again without looking."

This is not teaching spelling. Requiring that children memorize a list of "hard" words for the Friday test is not "rigor." Sad thing is, this kind of nonteaching of spelling (and vocabulary and grammar) goes on all the time in public schools, private schools—religious and secular—charter schools, fancy prep schools, and home schools. But this is not teaching spelling. Teaching spelling is teaching linguistic knowledge: rules, letter-sound reasons for the rules, reasons for words that don't follow the rules, letter clusters (patterns), and how related words tend to have similar letter clusters.

"I'm Just a Bad Speller"

Attributing spelling problems to "being a poor visual learner" is an oversimplification. Spelling, though learned primarily through the visual cues of reading, is also a thinking skill, even a logical one. Spelling is the byproduct of knowing about words, not just an exercise in rote memorization as some believe. If spelling were a matter of rote memorization, our Scripps-Howard Spelling Bee contestants would not know how to spell words that they have not seen before. They can spell such words, and they do it by applying rules and making informed guesses based on derivation and grammatical use. If a word has a Greek derivation, for example, it is likely to use the letter *y* in a place where the letter *i* would be used in a word with a Latin pedigree (e.g., *oxygen, mystery, dynasty, dystopia, lyric, physical, cycle*).

The Spelling Micro-Lesson

We are suggesting that you spend a very small but concentrated amount of time—not even a mini-lesson, more of a micro-lesson—linking spelling to meaning as you introduce your Tier III words. The micro-lesson in spelling is successful if it tightens the bond among what the Tier III word means, other words that it is related to, and maybe even *why* it is spelled the way it is.

The key to the micro-lesson is to ask, while you are teaching the meaning of the word, "What do we notice? What other words are spelled similarly?" It's hard to remember single bits of isolated information. It's much easier to remember meaning-related clusters. So we have to do everything we can to *create* these clusters, to *find* them. For example, in teaching the word *dynasty*, a teacher might say, "This is one of those words that has a y between two consonants. That means it comes into English from Greek. A lot of words that we learn about in school come from Greek and have that *y* between two consonants, like *cycle, tyranny, gyrate, mystery*. The Greek root *dyn* means power, like *dynamo* and *dynamic*. You might remember *A Dynasty Mystery*." That's your micro-lesson. It takes no more than a minute, and it establishes connections from the target word to other information.

Here's another micro-lesson, this time for that staple of social studies language, *civilization*: "Civilization is a long word, but it has parts that you know. What other words end in *–ization*?(*organization, colonization, fertilization*) Associate it with the words *civil, civilized, civilian, civics*, and *citizen*. It's actually related to the word *city*. What might be the connection between the words *city* and *civilization*?

Connecting Spelling to Meaning

Be that teacher who, in a matter of seconds at the board, delivers the rhyme and reason of spelling in a way that synergizes content and literacy. Revelations about the spelling-to-meaning connection can come to us through research (an unabridged dictionary is best) or through the intuitions about words that develop in your own mind as a result of a lifelong interest in learning about words and meaning. For example, I realized not too long ago that the word *college* (often misspelled) is created from the prefix *co* (with) to the root *leg* (to write). A few of its relatives are *legal, legislate, legible*, and *allege*. When we create clusters for students, we help them connect the meaning of a word to its spelling.

Assessing Spelling

Note that the standard calls for correct spelling in writing, not correct spelling in recitation, in a matching column, in a word find, or on a spelling test. Everyone who has ever given a spelling test knows that students can spell words on a test and then go right ahead and spell any old way where it counts, which is in writing. So let's skip the spelling tests altogether and assess students on the spelling that they do in writing. Doing so has the added benefit of elevating their vocabulary as they incorporate the required relevant words.

This kind of authentic assessment entails thinking about the kinds of words that are handy for upcoming writing assignments. When students write using Tier II and III words, they demonstrate content-area knowledge, academic vocabulary, and spelling knowledge.

Conclusion: Language

In social, business, and educational situations, we don't judge and measure a person's intelligence and competence by asking that person to solve a Rubik's cube. But language use is more than just an outward sign: Words, and how we put them together in speech and writing, are the very substance of thought in the human brain.

Fortunately, given the paramount importance of vocabulary, the human brain learns it naturally and effortlessly—if the words are presented in a way that reflects natural language acquisition: through rich and repeated context, and with opportunities to use new words for meaningful communication.

As for grammar and spelling, we advocate explicit instruction that 1) uses accurate terminology so that students and teachers can communicate in the "language of the language" and 2) emphasizes patterns. In addition to sound explicit instruction, teachers need to be aware that grammar and spelling are "caught, not taught" through the implicit modeling of reading and listening to language that we want students to learn.

CLASSROOM CLOSE-UPS for Language

A Picture Is Worth a Thousand Words ... Learned

Mrs. Jo-Ann Dellaposta is a veteran art teacher who makes use of literacy through her interactive instructional practices in her Studio-Photo I course. In her lesson plan below, the objective is for students to adjust the camera's shutter speed purposely in order to achieve "stop action," showing movement and panning. Students will adjust the camera's aperture in order to retain a normal exposure.

As you read, take note of her focus on literacy in the photography lesson and her use of content-specific vocabulary to drive the understanding of how the student photographer creates the desired effect for the photo.

Essential Question: What specific shutter-speed settings can we choose in order to achieve "stop action," showing movement and panning?

Activator/Do Now: Students read informational literature on the subject of controlling movement. Students underline or highlight any unfamiliar words.

Lesson procedure: Groups are formed and a scribe, the designated typist, is chosen from each group. Students build a vocabulary list of "words we need to know" from the reading. Each student shares the word or words that they underlined. As these content-specific (Tier III) words are revealed, the scribes type a list, which is usually 10–15 words long. Each student is given a word or two and is asked to look up a definition (they do this by using their iPhones or a computer). A teacher-generated list is later disseminated for all students as the unit of study progresses. After completing the list, students reread the text with the content-specific (Tier III) vocabulary definitions at hand.

Students work in pairs or teams to answer a number of critical-thinking questions about shutter speed that incorporate the vocabulary generated from the "words we need to know" list. Once complete, we return to whole-group instruction and, through the use of the interactive whiteboard, the answers to the questions are revealed and various scenarios of photography are presented for consideration. These scenarios promote higher-order thinking. Throughout the exercise, the students are encouraged to consult with their classmates for help.

Students are given the "final challenge." They have to apply the knowledge of shutter-speed mechanism to create a photo with the desired effect.

Lesson summarizer (Key Questions):

What camera function allows us to control subject movement? What shutter-speed setting can we use to "stop action," show movement, and use the panning technique? (Students are given a roll of film and asked to shoot it for homework, ultimately to print three separate photographs of "stopped action," showing movement and panning.)

Students must provide a written explanation of their thought process, delineating why they chose various settings to stop action and how they show movement and make use of panning techniques as they photograph. They must be able to justify their exposures and explain what happens when the shutter speed is increased or decreased.

This lesson is front loaded with vocabulary, reading, and engaging discussion, providing a foundational knowledge of the physical process of photography. Before they even touch a camera, students engage in the literature of photography and negotiate the content-specific (Tier III) vocabulary involved with the mechanisms of shutter speed, the processes of controlling movement and panning techniques. This lesson lends itself to an instructional model known as Situated Cognition or Cognitive Apprenticeship, whereby Mrs. Dellaposta's students must articulate their reasoning in writing (in this case, their understanding of how to apply techniques of photography) and then apply the theories learned in an apprentice situation to render a finished product (employ stop action, showing movement and panning to create a photo as the teacher scaffolds the physical application of the technique) (Lave, 1988).

It is important to note that the mindful approach of visualization, mentally working through a physical process, is incredibly powerful. Mrs. Dellaposta allows students to contemplate the processes and understand the act of photography in preparation for creating the photo. Most importantly, students make use of literacy and vocabulary as a vehicle for this practice, an initiative that accords with the foundations of the Common Core State Standards for Literacy. Let's further delineate the connections made to the CCSS in this lesson.

Mrs. Dellaposta's lesson engages a number of Anchor Standards from the CCSS for Reading, as her students are closely examining complex text, to follow a step-by-step process to create an effect in a photograph (Standards 1, 3, 10). As mentioned earlier, her students make connections with content-specific vocabulary and integrate knowledge as they visualize and mentally map the application of stop action, movement, and panning (Standards 5, 6, 7).

When students engage in the interactive component of the lesson, they satisfy all of the Language Anchor Standards for Vocabulary and Use (4–6). In addition, students get practice in summarizing and assessing the validity of information, while presenting information with the aid of digital media (Anchor Standards for Speaking and Listening 2–6). Finally, the writing component of the lesson facilitates the gathering of information from multiple sources to learn and apply the techniques and processes of photography (Anchor Standards for Writing 5, 8, 9).

Mrs. Dellaposta's literacy-fueled lesson creates opportunities to negotiate vocabulary, read, write and present about photography in preparation for students to employ new photographic techniques. Thus, literacy skills can be a precursor to a lesson in the technical subjects—all in congruence with the objectives set forth in the Common Core State Standards.

Whiteboard in Foreign Language Instruction

Mrs. Dali Rastello is currently assistant principal at Central Islip High School in Central Islip, New York. Previous to holding this position, Dali was a Spanish language teacher and department chairperson of the Foreign Language Department at Riverhead High School for over 20 years. She is an adjunct professor at a neighboring college and a master teacher with extensive knowledge about instruction and curriculum. Below, she describes her use of small washable whiteboards as a means to assess literacy skills in her classroom.

> The use of small white boards and markers encourages the most reluctant of learners to participate in a lesson. It allows the student who lacks confidence the anonymity necessary to take educational risks. It is also a wonderful tool to assess students' understanding, thought processes, and literacy skills.
>
> As a Spanish teacher, I use these small individual wipe-off boards to assess students' listening, writing, and grammar skills quite often. For example, if I want to activate prior learning for present-tense verb conjugations in the Spanish language, I ask students to conjugate a given verb on the whiteboard. Some students invariably finish earlier than others, so I take the opportunity to circulate the room, clarify confusion, and briefly assess student progress. After sufficient time elapses, I prompt students with a countdown (uno, dos, tres) to lift their boards and show their work simultaneously. After a quick glance around the room, I can determine which students have knowledge of the present-tense conjugation and which students still need some clarification.

At other times in lessons, I will sometimes have students turn to a partner to check for accuracy or compete for speed and race to write their answers and show the results. I vary the way in which I employ the whiteboards, depending on the difficulty of the task assigned.

Another way I use the boards is to assess student listening skills. I read a passage, show a part of a commercial or movie, or have students listen to a newscast or authentic conversation. Then I pause and ask comprehension questions based on what they just heard. Sometimes I differentiate the task by preparing three to four levels of questions on the chalkboard, on sentence strips, or on posters. The questions are labeled, and I assign students a question based on their ability. Questions are highlighted by different colors, numbers, or Spanish-speaking countries—anything more interesting than "John, Rachel and Laquan, answer questions from column A." Students will then document their answers on the erasable whiteboards. This allows me to assess students' writing ability instead of having them answer questions orally.

While I always incorporate literacy into each lesson, assessing students' skills by using the whiteboard in a creative, engaging, and nonthreatening manner allows me to check for understanding and facilitate individualized and productive lessons.

Here are some other ways in which I use the whiteboard activities with great success.

- Drawing the word they hear
- Answering questions—True (Cierto) or False (Falso)
- Checking for spelling
- Checking for correct translation of a word
- Checking for opinion about a story or conflict

We emphasize the importance of having students take academic risks in class, especially in a foreign language classroom. Note that Mrs. Rastello starts her discussion by pointing out the merits of the whiteboard as a tool to coax reluctant learners to participate in classroom activities. As a language learner, it is easier to passively observe, absorb, and understand a foreign tongue as opposed to actually speaking it. According to the language-acquisition theorist Stephen Kashen, this "silent period" is a time of transition from the known language to the new. However, it is during this developmental stage that interference with further language acquisition can occur should the learning environment become too volatile—as evidenced when a language teacher directs a student to speak the native tongue in a room full of his/her peers. Having a board to write on and show the instructor eases the pressure in the classroom and allows students to think, write, and make mistakes without fear of embarrassment. This "low anxiety" phenomenon, according to Kashen, is crucial in language acquisition (1981, p. 62). After all, the only person who is able to read every board in the room is the teacher. This fact alone eases pressure, encouraging students to take academic risks and answer a question they normally might not answer.

In addition to increased participation, Mrs. Rastello's use of the whiteboard for foreign-language instruction provides students the opportunity to hone skills in listening, writing, and reading. The use of the whiteboard provides for a range of writing in the native language as students are operating in the target language and negotiating the vocabulary in formal and informal contexts (Writing Anchor Standards 2, 5, 10).

The whiteboard also brings in listening and reading processes. As students are exposed to conversation or passages in the native language, they are developing the skills to read and listen closely, track themes, and follow progressions (Reading Anchor Standards 1–3; Listening Anchor Standards 1–3). In addition, as mentioned above, the whiteboard acts as a stepping stone to speaking in the target language, providing an avenue for student analysis and preparation to develop speaking skills of summarizing and presenting meaningful ideas coherently (Speaking Anchor Standard 4).

Mrs. Rastello's use of the whiteboard facilitates literacy. By bringing in literacy skill building in a nonthreatening manner, she can simultaneously facilitate the development skills in both the English and Spanish languages!

Conclusion

In "Most Teachers See the Curriculum Narrowing, Survey Finds," (*Curriculum Matters, Education Week's* blogs, December 8, 2011), we read the following:

> Most teachers believe that in the era of high-stakes testing in math and English/language arts, other important subjects are getting pushed out of the classroom. At the same time, nearly half of those polled believe the extra focus on math and English is helping to boost students' 'skills and knowledge' in one or both subjects.

I (Amy) think that both of these views are missing an important point: Education is not a zero-sum game, where time spent building skills in literacy and reasoning subtracts from time available to build skills and content in subjects that are not called English language arts and mathematics. In fact, building literacy and reasoning skills amplifies the learning capacity of students, thereby strengthening their ability to learn, remember, access, and process information throughout the school day and beyond.

Rather than seeing the Common Core as leaching time away from other subjects, we need to acknowledge and respond to the central importance that language and reasoning play in every subject. By infusing writing-to-learn activities, reinforcing academic vocabulary, and expecting students to access their own knowledge through content-area independent reading (and helping them do so), we are enriching education, not diluting it. The accurate use of language sharpens, almost defines, and even creates thinking skills.

If we do this thing correctly—not with worksheets, but with meaningful reading, writing, and vocabulary *experiences*—adherence to the Common Core will result in students who can express what they know and, equally important, what they don't know.

I wouldn't blame anyone who doesn't want to be that English teacher forever seen carrying around a worn old canvas bag stuffed with papers to grade. But teachers don't have to grade, edit, comment on, report, or even read everything students are asked to write. The real value of writing is to increase and refine knowledge for the writer, not the teacher. Writing does more than just express what you know. Writing actually creates what you know, allows you to see it.

Teachers are concerned about "finishing," the curriculum—which amounts to "covering" a set number of topics. If it were only a matter of that, we'd be giving workshops on how to talk faster. The real problem is that our students lack the capacity to access information on their own—the real problem is poor reading comprehension that results from 1) too slow a reading pace, the result of lack of practice, and 2) insufficient academic vocabulary, also the result of lack of practice. So in the absence of practice, here we are, stuck in a vicious cycle of having to teach around the fact that students are not up to the task of reading and writing as a means for learning. Because we don't require and help them to do so, we have to disseminate information ourselves, with our students as passive (and ineffective) learners.

Reading comprehension, vocabulary, and writing to learn affect all academic subjects. As for the arts, the incorporation of literacy-related experiences such as having small-group discussions and using technical language only enhances a student's proficiency and ability to participate in a community of like-minded artists. Most students in art and music classes are not going to become professional artists and performers. But we hope that they will invite art and music into their leisure lives as a means of pleasure and a vehicle for socialization.

Rather than exacerbating the need for remedial classes that actually do take away from electives, let's come at it another way: Let's have the electives provide the literacy supports that are inherent in learning those subjects. That would be much more motivating and effective than having students doing worksheets and practice tests in a remedial class.

APPENDIX A

Checklist for Paragraph Development

Checklist for Paragraph Development

I. Structure

- ☐ 1. Does the first sentence state the point of the paragraph, setting the reader up for the details and conclusion to follow?
- ☐ 2. Do the middle sentences give details such as reasons, explanations, examples, quotes, and facts?
- ☐ 3. Does the last sentence help us understand why we should be convinced, *or* why the ideas in the paragraph are important, *or* what is next?

II. Coherence

The sentences in the paragraph should stick together because you have done at least one of these things:

- ☐ 1. Did you repeat key words?
- ☐ 2. Do the last few words of each sentence set up the first few words of the next sentence?
- ☐ 3. Did you tie ideas together with conjunctions such as *and, but, so* and *after, as, although, when, while, until, because, before, if*?

III. Sentence Sense and Style

- ☐ 1. Is each sentence a complete sentence?
- ☐ 2. Are you sure that you have no run-on sentences?
- ☐ 3. Are you sure that you have not used the same word to begin several sentences, especially *and* or *then*?
- ☐ 4. Are you sure that you have not overused the following words, especially in sentence beginnings: *and, then, there is, there are, there was, there were, it is, it was*?
- ☐ 5. Have you expanded your vocabulary by using at least one word that you have not used before in writing?
- ☐ 6. Have you shown respect for the reader by writing neatly, proofreading, and using the kind of "formal school language" that appeals to the reader?

APPENDIX B

Writing Rubrics

Writing Rubric: Common Core State Standards, Grades 6–12:
English Language Arts — Type: Narrative

	PRE-NOVICE	NOVICE	SEMI-PRO	PRO
Writing an introduction	Does not succeed in engaging the reader; is vague and/or disorienting	Makes some noticeable attempt to engage the reader by establishing a setting, characters, and/or situation	Makes contact with the reader by establishing at least two of the following: character, setting, situation	Effectively engages and orients the reader by establishing a context and introducing a narrator and/or characters: organizes an event sequence that unfolds naturally and logically
Using narrative technique	No or little use of narrative techniques such as dialogue, description, pacing, characterization, conflict	Limited but noticeable use of more than one narrative technique, such as dialogue, pacing, description, characterization, conflict	Good start toward use of more than one narrative technique, such as dialogue, pacing, description, characterization, conflict	Engaging use of such narrative techniques as dialogue, pacing, description, characterization, conflict
Sequencing and transitioning	All or mostly simple sentences with no or very few transition words and conjunctions used; No paragraphing	Uses only the most basic transitional devices (words, punctuation, phrases, clauses, paragraphs) to convey shifts in time and space	Uses some transitional devices (words, punctuation, phrases, clauses, paragraphs, section divisions) to convey shifts in time and space	Uses a variety of transitional devices (words, punctuation, phrases, clauses, paragraphs, section division) to convey shifts in time and space
Vocabulary	Word choice does not show effort at being interesting and precise.	Glimmers of use of words that are interesting, lively, precise, accurate, striking, dramatic to create characters, setting, and conflict	Good start at using words that are interesting, lively, precise, accurate, striking, dramatic to create characters, setting, and conflict	Strong use of words that are interesting, lively, precise, accurate, striking, dramatic to create characters, setting, and conflict
Using formal writing tone	Overall tone is too informal, including some or all of: "texting" abbreviations, slang, messiness, errors in spelling, punctuation, grammar; no attempt to use dialect to capture the speech of the characters	Attempt at formal writing style, but needs more proofreading and/or care in presentation; attempt to use dialect to capture the speech of the characters	Good attempt at blending formal English conventions (spelling, grammar, punctuation, capitalization) with dialect to capture the speech of the characters	Excellent blend of formal English conventions (spelling, grammar, punctuation, capitalization) with dialect to capture the speech of the characters
Writing a conclusion	No or very sketchy conclusion	Some attempt at a conclusion that leaves the reader with a sense of closure	Good start toward a strong conclusion that leaves the reader with a sense of closure	Strong conclusion that rewards the reader for having read the story

Developed by Amy Benjamin in accordance with the Common Core State Standards for Literacy in English Language Arts and Social Studies, Science, Technical Subjects, www.amybenjamin.com

Writing Rubric: Common Core State Standards, Grades 6–12:

English Language Arts and Literacy for History, Social Studies, Science, and Technical Subjects — Type: Informational

	PRE-NOVICE	NOVICE	SEMI-PRO	PRO
Writing an introduction	Effectively does NEITHER of the following: Clarify the topic; Preview how it will be developed	Effectively does ONE of the following: Clarify the topic; Preview how it will be developed	Effectively does BOTH of the following: Clarify the topic; Preview how it will be developed	Effectively does BOTH of the following: Clarify the topic; Preview how it will be developed with headings and sub-headings
Explaining the information	No or few relevant facts, definitions, concrete details, quotations, examples	Some relevant facts, definitions, concrete details, quotations, examples	Good start toward presenting relevant facts, definitions, concrete details, quotations, examples	Thorough presentation of facts, including graphics such as well-explained charts, tables, and/or other visuals
Expressing relationships between ideas	All or mostly simple sentences with no or very few transition words and conjunctions used; No paragraphing	A few organizational structures and transitional words	Transitions from paragraph to paragraph, but needs more internal transition and linkage within paragraphs	Establishes clear and effective organization through paragraphing, sectioning, complex sentences, transitions and other linking devices
Using Tier II and III vocabulary	No Tier II or III vocabulary used	Some Tier II and III vocabulary used	Tier II and III vocabulary is evident, but there are several instances where Tier II vocabulary should be used instead of Tier I	Sufficient, appropriate use of Tier II and III language throughout
Language tone	Overall tone is too informal, including some or all of: "texting" abbreviations, slang, messiness, errors in spelling, punctuation, grammar	Attempt at formal writing style, but needs more proofreading and/or care in presentation	Good attempt at formal writing style and proofreading, but a few glaring errors indicate that more careful proofreading is needed	Formal writing tone used throughout; Few or no glaring errors in spelling, grammar, punctuation, capitalization; obvious care in presentation
Writing a conclusion	No or very sketchy conclusion	Some attempt at a conclusion that leaves the reader with a sense of closure	Good start toward a strong conclusion that explains the importance of the information	Strong conclusion that clearly summarizes the information and explains its importance
Developed by Amy Benjamin in accordance with the Common Core State Standards for Literacy in English Language Arts and Social Studies, Science, Technical Subjects, www.amybenjamin.com				

Writing Rubric: Common Core State Standards, Grades 6–12:

English Language Arts and Literacy for History, Social Studies, Science, and Technical Subjects — Type: Argumentation

	PRE-NOVICE	NOVICE	SEMI-PRO	PRO
Writing an introduction	Effectively does NONE of the following: State importance of issue; Make a claim; Acknowledge opposing claim(s)	Effectively does ONE of the following: State importance of issue; Make a claim; Acknowledge opposing claim(s)	Effectively does TWO of the following: State importance of issue; Make a claim; Acknowledge opposing claim(s)	Effectively does ALL of the following: State importance of issue; Make a claim; Acknowledge opposing claim(s)
Developing an argument	No relevant facts, statistics, reasons, or evidence	Mentions, but does not develop, sufficient evidence; Does not attend to opposing claim(s)	Good start toward developing claims and opposing claims; Includes some substantial evidence	Develops claims and opposing claims thoroughly and fairly with evidence: facts, stats, reasons, examples, anecdotes
Expressing relationships between ideas	All or mostly simple sentences with no or very few transition words and conjunctions used; No paragraphing	A few organizational structures and transitional words	Transitions from paragraph to paragraph, but needs more internal transition and linkage within paragraphs	Establishes clear and effective organization through paragraphing, sectioning, complex sentences, transitions and other linking devices
Using Tier II and III vocabulary	No Tier II or III vocabulary used	Some Tier II and III vocabulary used	Tier II and III vocabulary are evident, but there are several instances where Tier II vocabulary should be used instead of Tier I	Sufficient, appropriate use of Tier II and III language throughout
Using formal writing tone	Overall tone is too informal, including some or all of: "texting" abbreviations, slang, messiness, errors in spelling, punctuation, grammar	Attempt at formal writing style, but needs more proofreading and/or care in presentation	Good attempt at formal writing style and proofreading, but a few glaring errors indicate that more careful proofreading is needed	Formal writing tone used throughout; Few or no glaring errors in spelling, grammar, punctuation, capitalization; obvious care in presentation
Writing a conclusion	No conclusion	Sketchy conclusion that just restates the claim and/or the issue; does not make an impact on the reader	Good start toward a strong conclusion that follows from the evidence and makes an impact on the reader	Strong conclusion that follows from the evidence presented and makes an impact on the reader

Developed by Amy Benjamin in accordance with the Common Core State Standards for Literacy in English Language Arts and Social Studies, Science, Technical Subjects, www.amybenjamin.com

APPENDIX C

Academic Word List

Coxhead's Academic Word List

Subset 1: analyze, approach, area, assess, assume, authority, available, benefit, concept, consist, context, constitute, contract, data, define, derive, distribute, economy, environment, establish, estimate, evident, factor, finance, formula, function, income, indicate, individual, interpret, involve, issue, labor, legal, legislate, method, occur, percent, period, principle, proceed, process, policy, require, research, respond, role, section, sector, significant, source, specific, structure, theory, vary

Subset 2: achieve, acquire, administrate, affect, appropriate, aspect, assist, category, commission, complex, conduct, consequent, construct, consume, credit, culture, design, distinct, element, evaluate, feature, impact, institute, invest, maintain, obtain, perceive, positive, potential, previous, primary, range, region, regulate, relevant, reside, resource, restrict, secure, select, site, strategy, survey, tradition, transfer

Subset 3: alternative, circumstance, comment, compensate, component, consent, considerable, constant, constrain, contribute, convene, coordinate, core, corporate, correspond, criteria, deduce, demonstrate, document, dominate, emphasis, ensure, exclude, find, framework, illustrate, immigrate, imply, initial, instance, interact, justify, layer, link, maximize, negate, outcome, philosophy, physical, proportion, publish, react, register, rely, scheme, sequence, shift, specify, sufficient, technical, technique, valid, volume

Subset 4: access, adequacy, annual, apparent, approximate, attitude, attribute, civil, code, commit, concentrate, confer, contrast, cycle, debate, despite, dimension, domestic, emerge, ethnic, grant, hence, hypothesis, implement, implicate, impose, integrate, internal, investigate, mechanism, occupy, option, output, overall, parallel, parameter, phrase, prior, principal, professional, project, promote, regime, resolve, retain, series, statistic, status, stress, subsequent, undertake

Subset 5: academy, adjust, alter, amend, capacity, clause, compound, consult, decline, discrete, enable, energy, enforce, entity, equivalent, evolve, expand, expose, external, facilitate, fundamental, generate, liberal, license, logic, margin, modify, monitor, network, notion, objective, orient, perspective, precise, prime, psychology, pursue, ratio, reject, revenue, stable, style, substitute, sustain, symbol, target, transit, trend, version, welfare, whereas

Subset 6: abstract, acknowledge, accuracy, aggregate, allocate, assign, bond, capable, cite, cooperate, discriminate, display, diverse, domain, edit, enhance, estate, exceed, explicit, federal, fee, flexible, furthermore, gender, incentive, incorporate, incidence, index, inhibit, initiate, input, interval, mitigate, minimum, ministry, motive, neutral, nevertheless, overseas, precede, presume, rational, recover, reveal, scope, subsidy, trace, transform, underlie, utilize

Subset 7: adapt, advocate, channel, classic, comprehensive, comprise, confirm, contrary, convert, decade, deny, differentiate, dispose, dynamic, equip, eliminate, empirical, extract, finite, foundation, gradient, guarantee, hierarchy, identical, ideology, infer, innovate, insert, intervene, isolate, media, mode, paradigm, phenomenon, priority, prohibit, publication, quote, release, reverse simulate, sole, somewhat, submit, successor, thesis, transmit, ultimate, unique, voluntary

Subset 8: abandon, accompany, accumulate, ambiguous, appendix, appreciate, arbitrary, automate, bias, chart, clarify, commodity, complement, conform, contemporary, contradict, crucial, currency, denote, detect, deviate, displace, eventual, exhibit, exploit, fluctuate, guideline, implicit, induce, inevitable, infrastructure, inspect, intense, manipulate, minimize, nuclear, offset, predominant, prospect, radical, reinforce, restore, revise, tension, terminate, theme, thereby, uniform, vehicle, via, virtual, widespread

Subset 9: accommodate, analogy, anticipate, assure, attain, behalf, cease, coherent, coincide, commence, compatible, concurrent, confine, controversy, converse, device, devote, diminish, distort, duration, erode, ethic, found, format, inherent, insight, integral, intermediate, manual, mature, mediate, medium, military, minimal, mutual, norm, overlap, passive, portion, preliminary, protocol, qualitative, refine, restrain, revolution, rigid, route, scenario, sphere, subordinate, supplement, suspend, trigger, unify, violate

Subset 10: adjacent, albeit, assemble, collapse, colleague, compile, conceive, convince, depress, encounter, forthcoming, incline, integrity, intrinsic, invoke, levy, likewise, nonetheless, notwithstanding, ongoing, panel, persist, pose, reluctance, so-called, straightforward, undergo, whereby

APPENDIX D

Semantic Features Chart

Semantic Features Chart
Common Word Endings of the Elements

SEMANTIC FEATURES CHART Common Word Endings of the Elements				
-ium	**-on**	**-gen**	**-ine**	**-y**
helium, lithium, beryllium, sodium, magnesium, potassium, calcium, scandium, titanium, vanadium, chromium, gallium, germanium, selenium, rubidium, strontium, yttrium, zirconium, niobium, technetium, ruthenium, rhodium, palladium, cadmium, indium, tellurium, cesium, barium, cerium, praseodymium, neodymium, promethium, samarium, europium, gadolinium, terbium, dysprosium, holmium, erbium, thulium, ytterbium, lutetium, hafnium, rhenium, osmium, iridium, thallium, polonium, francium, radium, actinium, thorium, protactinium, uranium, neptunium, plutonium, americium, curium, berkelium, californium, einsteinium, fermium, mendelevium, nobelium, lawrencium, rutherfordium, dubinium, seaborgium, borhium, hassium, meiterium, darmstadium, roetgenium, copernicium, ununtrium, ununquadium, ununpentium, ununhexium, unundeptium, ununcoctium	boron, carbon, neon, silicon, argon, iron, krypton, xenon, radon	hydrogen, nitrogen, oxygen	fluorine, chlorine, bromine, iodine, astatine	antimony, mercury **other:** sulfur, cobalt, nickel, copper, zinc, arsenic, silver, tin, lead, platinum, gold, bismuth, aluminum

References

Alliance for Excellence in Education. Issue Brief. 2006. http://www.all4ed.org/publication_material/fact_sheets/AdLit_FactSheet

Anderson, L. W., & Krathwohl, D. R. (Eds.). (2001). *A Taxonomy for learning, teaching and assessing: A revision of Bloom's Taxonomy of Educational Objectives*: Complete edition, New York : Longman.

Armstrong, S. (2008). *Teaching smarter with the brain in focus: Practical ways to apply the latest brain research to deepen comprehension, improve memory, and motivate students to achieve.* New York: Scholastic.

Beck, Isabel, Margaret G. McKeown, and Linda Kucan (2002). *Bringing words to life: Robust vocabulary instruction.* New York: Guilford.

Benjamin, Amy and Joan Berger (2008). *Grammar instruction: What really works.* Larchmont, New York: Eye On Education.

Benjamin, Amy and John T. Crow (2008, 2012). *Vocabulary at the core: Teaching the Common Core standards.* Larchmont, New York: Eye On Education.

Blaine, Ray. *Total physical response storytelling.* www.blaineraytprs.com.

Brophy, Jere E., and Thomas L Good. *Looking in classrooms.* New York: Longman, 1997.

Cazden, Courtney B (2001). *Classroom discourse: The language of teaching and learning.* Portsmouth, New Hampshire: Heinemann.

Chickering, A. W., & Schlossberg, N. K. (1995). *Getting the most out of college.* Upper Saddle, NJ: Prentice Hall.

Coxhead, Averil. The AWL (Academic Word List) Composed in 2000 by Averil Coxhead (TESOL Quarterly, 34, 218-238).

Deye, Sunny. "A Path to Graduation for Every Child." National Council of State Legislatures. Retrieved June 20, 2012 from http://www.ncsl.org/documents/educ/NCSLDropoutTaskForceReport.pdf.

www.Engageny.com

Fisher, Douglas, Nancy Frey and Dianne Lapp (2012). *Text complexity: Raising rigor in reading*. Newark, Delaware: International Reading Association.

Florida, Richard."Where the Skills Are." *The Atlantic Magazine*. July 12, 2012.

Gibbs, John, Bud Potter Granville, and Arnold P. Goldstein. *The EQUIP Program (1995). Teaching Youth to Think and Act Responsibly*. Champaign, Illinois: Research Press.

Gladwell, Malcolm. (June 3, 1996). "The Tipping Point." From *The New Yorker*. Retrieved from http://www.gladwell.com/1996/1996_06_03_a_tipping.htm.

Goldstein, Arnold. *The PREPARE Curriculum: Teaching Prosocial Competencies* (1999). Champaign, Illinois: Research Press.

Graff, David, Cathy Birkenstein, and Russell Durst (2006). *They say/I say: The moves that matter in academic writing*. New York, New York: W. W. Norton and Company.

Grubb, W. N. (1999). *Honored but invisible: An inside look at teaching in community colleges*. New York, NY: Routledge

Hightower, Dirk A. and Emory Cowen (1995). School-Based Prevention for Children at Risk. Primary Mental Health Project. American Psychological Association.

Hillocks, G., Jr., 1986. *Research on written composition: New directions for teaching.* ED 265552. Urbana, Ill.: ERIC

"Improving College Completion. Reforming Remedial Education. Retrieved June 20, 2012 from http://www.ncsl.org/issues-research/educ/improving-college-completion-reforming-remedial.aspx.

Jensen, Eric (1995). *The learning brain*. Delmar, California: Turning Point.

Kesselman-Turkel, J. & Peterson, F. (1981). *Test-taking strategies*. Chicago, Illinois: Contemporary Books, Inc.

Knoff, Howard M. "Stop and Think" Social Skills Program (2001). Sopris West.

Krashen, S. (1981). *Bilingual Education and Second Language Acquisition Theory.* In California State Department of Education (Ed.), *Schooling and Language Minority Students: A Theoretical Framework*. Los Angeles, California: Evaluation, Dissemination and Assessment Center, California State University.

Krashen, Stephen D. http://www.sdkrashen.com/Principles_and_Practice/index.html. accessed August, 2012.

Krashen, Stephen D. (2004). *The power of reading*. Portsmouth, New Hampshire: Heinemann.

Lave, J. (1988). *Cognition in practice: Mind, mathematics, and culture in everyday life*. Cambridge, United Kingdom: Cambridge University Press.

Lyman, Frank. Think-pair-share (1981) University of Maryland.

Marzano, Robert J., Debra Pickering and Jane E. Pollack. *Classroom strategies that work* (2004). Boston, Massachusetts: Prentice Hall.

McCallister, Cynthia. *Unison reading: Socially inclusive group instruction for equity and achievement (2011)*. Thousand Oaks, California: Corwyn.

McCrorie, Ken. www.delta.edu/sgrobins/I-Search.html. Accessed August, 2012.

National Association of School Psychologists. http://www.nasponline.org/resources/factsheets/socialskills_fs.aspx (NASP Fact Sheet—Social Skills). accessed August, 2012.

National Governors Association Center for Best Practices & Council of Chief State School Officers. (2010). Common Core State Standards for English language arts and literacy in history/social studies, science, and technical subjects. Washington, DC: Authors, Retrieved June 20, 2012, from www.corestandards.org/the-standards.

Pascual-Leone, A., & Baillargeon, R. (1994). Developmental Measurement of Mental Attention. *International Journal of Behavioral Development*, 17, 161–200.

"Starting Off Strong." The Great Book Foundation. www.greatbooks.org/programs-for-all-ages/.../starting-off-strong/. Accessed August, 2012.

Sylwester, R. (2005). *How to explain a brain: An educator's handbook of brain terms and cognitive processes.* Thousand Oaks, CA: Corwin Press.

Trelease, Jim, quoted in *Readicide: How schools are killing reading and what you can do about it* (2009). Kelly Gallagher. Portland, Maine: Stenhouse.

Wenning, Carl, "Whiteboarding and Socratic Dialogue: Questions and Answers. *Journal of Physics Teacher Education Online*, 3 (1) September 2005.

NOTES

NOTES

NOTES